MONEY: THE VIRGIN GUIDE

Samantha Downes

First published in Great Britain in 2003 by
Virgin Books Ltd
Thames Wharf Studios
Rainville Road
London
W6 9HA

A catalogue record for this book is available from the British Library.

ISBN 0 7535 0745 5

Typeset by Phoenix Photosetting, Chatham, Kent
Printed and bound in Great Britain by Mackays of Chatham, Kent

CONTENTS

Also published by Virgin Books:

Buying a Home: The Virgin Guide
Dating: The Virgin Guide
Entertaining: The Virgin Guide

WHY READ THIS BOOK?

BECAUSE...

£ **managing money successfully is one of the most empowering things you can do**

£ **managing the cash you do have – and managing the money you don't – is easier than you think**

£ **good money management can make for better relationships**

£ **you *can* afford it – you just need to learn how**

£ **you don't need to spend another sleepless night worrying about money**

A NATION OF FINANCIAL DUNCES?

At school we were taught how to write proper sentences, how to add up, learn French/German/Latin, paint, cook, and even how to make cute-looking – and maybe not so cute-looking – animal shapes from bits of wood. Yet somehow in the midst of all this we missed out on one of the most valuable life skills: how to manage money.

Don't blame teachers, or your parents – in the last ten years credit cards, student loans, mortgages, overdrafts, buying and selling shares have become ingrained into our everyday lives in a way our parents, grandparents or people of their generations couldn't have imagined. And it's only in the last few years that schools and the government have wised up to the fact that children need to be equipped to face the daily, monthly and yearly slings and arrows of financial fortune and misfortune.

DON'T WORRY ABOUT MONEY

There are still an awful lot of us in the world who are paralysed by fear when it comes to all things cash-related. No wonder: we are constantly bombarded with contradictory advice on where to put, and where not to put, our money.

In fact, many of us probably put off decisions about money, such as taking out a pension or saving, simply because we don't really understand exactly what it is we'll get at the end of it all.

And then there are all those other nagging money worries: Are we saving enough? Should we really still be renting? Should we be buying shares? Could we be using our money to go into business? Is the savings account the right one for us?

Being comfortable with cash and knowing that you're doing your best to make the most of what you've got and to enjoy what you have is the aim of this book.

You don't have to go back to school, or be stingy, in order to make the most of your cash.

What you can learn to do is:

£   **face up to debt and do something about paying it off**
£   **work out the good debts from the bad debts**
£   **learn to save – and invest**
£   **stop money issues ruining relationships**
£   **protect yourself and your family from financial misfortune**
£   **get the most out of your job**
£   **realise that lots of other people are in the same 'money boat' as you**

HOW TO USE THIS BOOK

To make it easy on you, the book is divided into chapters that deal with nearly everything you need to know about money, using inspiring tales of people who've 'been there, done that'.

It also explains a lot of the jargon used by financial companies. They are not being awkward by using these long-winded words and weird phrases: it's just that, with government regulation on investments, savings, pensions and borrowing being quite strict, advisers and other experts have to use the correct terms for things.

There's also a **Resources** section containing useful names, numbers and websites that you can add to your new, financially savvy address book.

1 SPENDING IT

With someone else's money: credit cards, loans and other borrowings

It's a dilemma all but the most financially virtuous of us are familiar with. You're strolling through an upmarket department store and you spot 'it'.

We're not talking about Jennifer Aniston and Brad Pitt, although, as one of the world's most fabulous couples, they do qualify as a single entity. No, this is something more than star spotting: this is the dress/coat/sofa/lipstick that you suddenly can't be without.

There's no question in your mind about its usefulness or its practicality – you simply have to have it. You think about it, mulling over exactly how you are going to manage without something whose existence was revealed to you only ten minutes before.

You try to get back to the rational world where 'it' doesn't really matter. You go for a coffee and wander around with your eyes glazed over while you do a mental recce on how you can get your hands on the cash to buy it without resorting to something illegal: you haven't got enough money in your bank account and eating into your savings (what savings?) is a no-no.

And then, through the fog of your self-induced retail high, you suddenly remember that shiny bit of plastic that never says no – your credit card.

Scary fact: most of the money we spend is actually someone else's, and we're getting away with it – entirely legally.

With our busy, crazy lives and work eating into a sizeable chunk of everyday existence, it's easy to justify spending hard-earned cash on luxuries that make things a little bit more luxurious – and bearable. There's no longer a reason say, 'I can't afford it', because somewhere someone is prepared to lend you the cash to fulfil your retail whims.

IT'S NOT ALL BAD

It's inevitable that there will be times when credit is necessary: for a new washing machine or a bed – as well as a gorgeous sofa. The real dilemma becomes not what you spend, but what kind of debt you take on.

There are more than two thousand credit cards, hundreds of loan companies and hundreds of store cards, all with charges and interest that can bedazzle the most financially savvy. It doesn't pay to be complacent – as Kerri, a trainee analyst at a city investment bank found out. 'I'd been persuaded to take out a store card when I needed a dress for my firm's posh drinks do,' she says. 'I spent two hundred pounds and basically forgot about it. But, because I'd signed a direct-debit form that allowed the shop to take a minimum payment out of my account, I didn't get into trouble. When I bothered to check my statement I saw that I'd eventually ended up paying nearly four hundred pounds – that's about two hundred pounds in interest. And I thought I was dead smart when it came to money.'

WHAT'S THE RIGHT KIND OF CREDIT FOR YOU?

CREDIT CARDS

Stephen Hawking, eat your heart out: there's already a marvellous form of time travel available right here, right now – the credit card. This piece, or pieces of, plastic can take your finances forward a few weeks by allowing you to borrow ahead of pay day. But like all applications of science it needs to be used wisely, or you may end up with your own Frankenstein – a big scary debt.

What is a credit card? Credit cards give you a financial breathe-easy period of four to six weeks. They are also a fantastic money-spinner for those who issue them because very few of us actually pay off the full balance within those six weeks. We are more likely to pay off a bit, and then spend our remaining credit limit on something else. If this happens month on month, then the interest can soon tot up.

That said, credit cards are handy for spreading expensive purchases over two pay cheques, if you can be disciplined in paying it back. Also, there are some advantages to whacking it on plastic: some credit cards come with free insurance, so if the goods you buy are faulty or stolen – within reason – you can get them replaced or your money refunded.

How much can I spend? Anything from £200 to £20,000.

How do I pay it back? You receive a monthly statement that tells you when and for how much the minimum payment should be made; this is also the same date you need to bear in mind if you don't want to pay interest. If you can't pay back the full balance, you'll be charged interest on the unpaid bit, so if you spend £800 but only pay back £400 you'll have to pay interest on the remaining £400.

Can I just make the minimum payment? Making a minimum payment – £5 or 3 per cent of the balance you owe, whichever is the greater – is a good idea only if you are really, really strapped for cash. 'I have my own minimum payment and it's always about four times more than the kind the credit card is asking for. So if they ask for £20 I'll pay £80,' says Sarah, a dancer who's retrained as a financial adviser.

Frightening fact There's another good reason to pay it back. The Financial Services Authority, a government body set up to oversee the finance industry, has a scary sum to prove how expensive credit cards can be. If you have a debt of £1,000 with an interest rate of 18 per cent a year; and you pay off only the minimum balance each month, the FSA says it would take you thirteen years to pay off the whole balance and your repayments would total £1,772. That's £772 that could be spent on other things, and if you're using it to make new purchases it could end up being even longer.

How the interest rate is worked out What you end up paying back on top of your balance is called the *annual percentage rate* or APR. The APR includes the interest you pay and the annual fee you also may have to pay, although not all credit cards have annual fees. If you are looking at other kinds of credit, such as a loan or a store card (see below), you should be able to compare the APRs safely. Warning, though: a card with a lower APR is cheaper than a card with a higher APR – but the APR does not take into account extra charges you may have to pay, such as those imposed for missing your monthly repayment.

Credit-card companies get their kicks from luring customers away from competitors; many card issuers offer introductory interest rates that can be as low as zero per cent for the first six months. Always check the small print when you sign up for one of these, though, because it applies only to any balance you transfer from another card, not necessarily to any new purchases you make after the transfer. And your repayments will still be applied to the balance you transfer and not just anything you spend money on during the introductory period. So, you will still have to keep up the minimum repayments on the balance, whatever interest rate it is.

Credit-card whoring This doesn't mean paying for prostitutes by credit card – it's a little less racy than that. This new phenomenon is where canny consumers transfer the balance of their credit card to another credit card for a lower interest rate, and as soon as that introductory period runs out (see above) switch their balance to another card offering a low rate. The lower interest rate is made available by credit cards to encourage customers to put more money on their card. This interest rate may be as low as zero per cent. Again, that zero per cent will probably apply for only six months, so that after the six months has expired you'll be expected to pay a higher rate of interest. Remember that these types of deal rely on our inability to pay off the balance in six months.

Is interest all I'll pay? You may also be expected to pay an annual fee for the privilege of having a credit card. And this, like the interest rate, can vary – as Mark, a software designer found out. 'I took out two credit cards, with different credit-card companies,' he says. 'Both seemed to be charging exactly the same rate of interest when I took them out.

'When I first got them I decided to buy a laptop and split the cost, a thousand pounds, between the two cards. Somehow I ended up paying two very different amounts, even when I owed the same money: five hundred pounds. What it came down to was the way the interest rate was calculated – and the fee for having the cards in the first place. It just shows how complicated cards can be.'

Platinum, gold, silver or black? Credit-card companies want you to feel special, so they have different sorts of credit card, depending on how much you spend, how much you earn and what occupation you are in. For every credit card there are at least three, maybe four, different colours. Always compare APRs of different cards before you decide which one to get. What your credit card gives you with one hand, such as free life insurance, could be taken away with the other in terms of interest or charges.

Charity or affinity credit cards For every pound you spend on your charity card a set amount is donated to the charity or organisation – such as a trade union – in whose name you have taken the account. Remember, though, that charity credit cards do charge higher rates of interest.

'I took out a card on behalf of a really big UK charity, but it only worked out that I was donating about twenty-five pence for every fifty pounds I spent. I ended up cancelling the card and just setting up a standing order instead,' said Paul, a 32-year-old teacher.

But if your idea of retail therapy is about putting something back into the world, and you don't mind paying more interest, then go ahead. As a committed environmentalist, Sarah, a nursery nurse, did just that. 'I've always supported Greenpeace,' she says, 'and I spend a lot on my card, so I don't mind the fact the interest is a bit more than I'd usually pay.'

Gimmicks – are they for real? Well, you wouldn't stick your nose up at the chance of acquiring free holiday insurance, points to spend in your favourite shop, even discounts on theatre and cinema tickets and, in a few cases, free healthcare cover.

The more you spend on your credit card, the nicer your credit company will be to you. But even for all these gimmicks there's really only one thing you should be checking out, and that's how much interest you have to pay.

Who works out my credit limit? Your credit rating (explained below) will affect your ability to get a credit card. Your credit limit is based on your credit rating. How you manage your card – how much you spend on it and how swiftly you repay your balance – will determine by how much your credit limit is increased. You can up your limit. In fact, if you aren't spending very much or are paying the balance back regularly, the card company will very often raise it automatically, as Vicki, a PhD student in chemistry, found out. She'd had a credit card since her first week at college but only really wanted to use it when she was working. 'I got given a credit card in freshers' week at university,' she says. 'I hardly spent anything on it for the following three years, during which time the bank upped my limit from four hundred to eight hundred pounds. Of course, once I graduated, that eight hundred pounds came in very, very handy.'

Minus points on your credit card That shiny new plastic with the promise of £2,000 to spend is so tempting, and it takes a brave man or woman not to overindulge – but you can manage them, and here's how:

£   Be regular. Make regular repayments by direct debit and pay back more than the minimum balance. If you wish, you can pay your card off by using your bank debit card over the phone, or over a secure Internet site – make sure the site has a padlock symbol on the right-hand side of the page, though, as this tells you you're using a secure link.

£   For emergencies only. Credit cards come into their own when used for business expenses. When abroad, using a credit card can sometimes save you cash. Iain, an accountant who wanted to spend some money on his wardrobe during a business trip, explained: 'In the US on a business trip I took my credit card and paid for nearly all the designer gear I picked up on plastic. Apparently I saved about a hundred pounds on a thousand pounds' worth of things.'

£   Thinking big. Putting a large purchase such as a piece of furniture on a credit card is an idea (it could be that sofa again or maybe a stereo or something for the kitchen). Buying something on a Visa card means it is automatically covered by insurance. And, of course, if you are a spendthrift, buying on your card will, via your card statement, give you a great record of when, on what and how much you spent.

Credit enemies

£   Don't go too low. Try to pay more than the minimum balance. If you cannot pay off the bill in full always try to pay as much as you can.

£   Shop, shop, shop. Try to shop around for credit cards and make sure you get one with the lowest APR possible – that means you're paying less interest.

STORE CARDS

'I can never forget the day I got my sticky mitts on a store card for a well-known Oxford Street department store. I went crazy. My limit was four hundred pounds, so I used up that four hundred. Then I got a store card for a well-known fashion chain and I used that limit up, too. I was like a kid in a sweet shop – well, make that a very expensive sweet shop. It was fabulous until I got my bills through: then it was like that sickly, or what my nan called that liverish, feeling you get when you know you've overindulged.' So speaks Joanne. She may be cured of her store-card addiction but there are still plenty of people out there who think that using their store card is not like spending real money.

Before we start ... Store cards are a luxurious and enjoyable way of spending your money. And remember: it is still your money. Having a store card as a status symbol – Harvey Nichols, Selfridges, Harrods – is great so long as you can pay the balance off regularly. Oh, and when you do take out a store card, check the interest rate: it may be better to pop your purchases on your credit card.

Store crazy? A store card is probably the most expensive way of borrowing cash. They often have twice the interest rate of credit cards. Store cards are best avoided or used very sparingly.

Still want a store card? They do have their uses, though. If you are loyal to one particular high street chain then having a store card may give you special discounts not available to ordinary shoppers. Store-card holders often get exclusive preview evenings, too.

Charge cards versus store cards Some stores offer charge cards. These are not to be confused with normal store cards. A charge card is something you *have* to pay off in full every time you receive a statement. There are some charge cards that allow you to pay off every quarter, some even every six months. But often with these you have to spend quite a large amount.

Store-card and charge-card plus points

£   You may qualify for special offers, such as discounts and late shopping nights.
£   You may get a reduction for paying your balance by direct debit.

Minus points

£ The interest rate is usually higher than that of credit cards.
£ You can use them to buy things only in certain shops.
£ With a charge card you will have to pay the entire balance back each month.
£ The special offers might increase your temptation to overspend.

Interest rates explained Hands up those who haven't ever been approached by an oh-so-friendly shop assistant asking if you'd like to take out a store card.

'Well I've been in a lot of credit-card trouble in the past, so I'm now quite wised up to interest rates and charges,' says Marianne, a 33-year-old computer trainer and software designer, and someone who reads the small print. 'The woman with the sweet smile and the cloying perfume was quite surprised when I asked her what the rate of interest on the card was – it was a whopping twenty-two per cent. The reason she was surprised was that, out of all the people she'd asked, even those who had taken the card out, I was the only one who checked.'

How is the interest rate calculated? Store cards also use APRs to let you know how much it is you'll be paying off. But, again, comparing two different store cards can be tough because it may not take into account other charges, such as those imposed for missing a repayment.

OVERDRAFTS

Also known as 'going into the red', an overdraft is an extension of your current account, and is the most common form of debt. You know you're overdrawn because your statement will have the capitals OD or a minus sign next to your account details. Overdrafts can be a great way to cover for lack of cash, especially at the end of the month if you have to pay an urgent bill but don't quite have the readies. Many banks encourage you to go into the red by offering free £50–100 credit zones that allow us to dip into in overdraft for a few days a month.

Overdrafts are really only for people who can handle the possibility that sometimes they might still end up in the red, even after their salary has gone in. Psychologically, overdrafts are the easiest debts to draw up: they don't look expensive – because banks don't charge as much interest as on a loan – and they don't affect your cash flow because you don't have to make regular repayments to clear them. You could indeed spend your whole life overdrawn and your bank wouldn't care. Why should they? You are, after all, still paying them for the privilege of using their cash.

Your overdraft – what is it good for?

£   bills you have to pay when you're running near to empty
£   an unexpected expense or an emergency while you're abroad
£   if you're disciplined with cash and know you can pay it off each month

And bad for?

£   the financially undisciplined
£   those who think 'it's not real money' – but you still have to pay it off at the end of the day
£   using to spend on fripperies

FINANCIAL FIRST AID FOR PEOPLE NEEDING TO PAY OFF AN OVERDRAFT

The cheapest way to borrow cash – not! 'My overdraft has been with me since I left college,' says James, a 36-year-old plumber. 'Of course, it was free then, but in my first year of work, what with all the expenses and everything, it ended up getting higher and higher. The bank were very kind, or seemed to be. My first year, the overdraft was free.

'Then, just about the time it hit two thousand pounds, the bank started charging me interest. Of course it seemed cheaper than a loan. I've sometimes gone over it, too, and that means a twenty-five-pound penalty for going over my authorised limit.

'I've had the overdraft for fifteen years and, now I'm paying a mortgage, it doesn't look like I'll be paying it off any time soon. If in the beginning I had worked out how much interest I'd paid on the overdraft it would probably have worked out cheaper to get a loan, as I haven't got the discipline to pay off the overdraft.'

Over your limit This is the true rub, as Shakespeare would say. It's all very well keeping within your limit, but once you go over expect the bank to become heavy-handed. Some banks will charge £50 as soon as you go one penny over the agreed amount, and will often increase the interest, too.

We've all been there, and there's no real substitute for keeping an eye on your bank balance. So make that a promise to yourself – as well as vowing that you'll read this book, of course! Chances are there may be some expenses you can put off till next month, such as that big night out you had planned. You don't have to deprive yourself: just keep an eye on your account.

In the red – again Overdrafts are almost forgivable but it's no good for your state of mind to see your monthly salary just about bringing your balance into the black only for it to go into the red again. You have got to think about the effect your overdraft is having on your spending habits. Are you starting to say 'what the hell!' a lot more when you spy an unnecessary but oh-so-gorgeous item of clothing? If you are, it really may be time to rein in your spending and your overdraft.

How do I pay off an overdraft? Take a deep breath, grab a coffee, or a glass of the strong stuff.

You also need:

£   a large dose of willpower
£   a decent bank
£   and a bit of budgeting

You have to start treating your overdraft as a loan, one that is repayable in small doses. Stop promising yourself that you'll pay it all off in one go. Be realistic: if your overdraft is £2,000 you'll need to stagger it.

Steps to paying off your overdraft Remember that the only person who can pay off your overdraft is you – your bank is very unlikely to suggest that you do, unless you have been very bad about managing your account.

£   Let your bank know that you want your overdraft limit reduced by, say, £50 per month and arrange to do this on pay day, when it won't seem quite so frightening.
£   We'll also assume you haven't been too bad and your bank isn't demanding you pay off your overdraft straightaway.

£   Remember you need to start on a manageable amount because you'll
     have to reduce your spending by that amount: £50 is normally good to
     stick to, but if you feel you can go for £100 – brave you! – then do so.
£   Budget – and this is where your willpower will come in. Your bank will
     probably be more than pleased if, three weeks into your overdraft-
     repayment plan, you suddenly decide that you can't hack it and bring
     your overdraft back to square one. That's how they make money.

Budgeting This is all about deciding where the cash is going to be
sliced off from your budget. If you can't for the life of you think of
how you're going to get your spending down, then you are going to
have to resort to a very brutal piece of financial surgery, writing
down everything you spend – be it on tea bags, lattes, glasses (or
bottles) of wine – for a month. Then take a long, slow look. A latte
from Coffee Republic/Starbucks/Costa every morning can work out
at about £14 a week; or, if you get two (like me), then that's £28. Cut
back on that for a month and you could save yourself over £100.

There are other expenses, such as food. Ready-made meals end up
swallowing much more money than home cooking does. Even if you
can manage to make only two meals a week you could end up
shaving another £5. Think of swapping to own-brand supermarket
food, such as tinned tomatoes or pasta.

The shock treatment for when you really can't pay it off OK, so
you've tried willpower and it got you nowhere. Here's the short,
sharp, shock version that's been tried and tested: go for a cash-
only current account.

These were bank accounts originally designed for the financially
challenged, for people with very low or nonexistent credit ratings.
Essentially, these accounts do have cash (ATM) and debit cards, but
they are normally run by either Solo or Visa Electron. These cards
use different technology that is instantly able to access your bank-
account details and that means you can't go overdrawn. Your bank
will normally let you operate such an account alongside your
normal current account.

If you really want to pay off your overdraft, freeze your current
account and open the cash-only version. Your bank should allow you
to transfer your standing orders to that account, but you won't have
a cheque card or a normal debit card. Then have your salary paid

into the new account but arrange for a said amount of money to pay off the current-account overdraft via a standing order. Because you've frozen your current account you won't be able to up your overdraft limit once you've started paying it off. Pretty drastic, eh?

'I ended up with a three-thousand-pound overdraft – there was no way of paying it off,' says 25-year-old Yasmin. 'After one Christmas when I got so sick with stress over money I decided to ask my bank for some advice. They came up with the idea of opening what they called an instant-plus account. It worked like a bank account, so I could have standing orders and direct debits paid out of it, but I didn't have a cheque book, so I couldn't go overdrawn. It was a good discipline to have. Two years later I'm less stressed and I don't have an overdraft.'

LOANS

These are strictly for the long term. The difference is that you choose how long you take to pay back your debt: anything from a year to ten years. Smaller amounts can be repaid in as little as one year. Larger amounts can be paid back over ten years.

Who offers loans? Time was when banks and building societies were the only lenders in town. Now there is a plethora of companies wanting to lend you cash. In fact even supermarkets such as Tesco and Sainsbury and Marks & Spencer are now in on the act. Add to that some of the credit cards – Barclaycard, for example – and you have an awful lot of choice.

Buy-now-pay-later loans A common form of loan, also known as hire purchase, is the kind when you buy something from a shop and it offers you credit. The shop still has to go to a bank to offer this kind of finance, so it is in effect an agent of the bank. A credit agreement may have cheaper repayments or even nonexistent repayments for a special introductory period – but it may work out more expensive because they are often paid off over a longer period. Remember that, if you have a loan with the shop, under the 1979 Sale of Goods Act the bank has equal responsibility, along with the shop, for the quality of the goods you buy. Make sure you get a decent guarantee when you do buy, with or without a credit agreement.

Here's a cautionary tale from Colin, who got his fingers burned when buying a washing machine. 'My wife and I went to one of those discount stores where you can buy nearly-new things. They offered us credit – six months free, then three years' payments. The thing is, the machine only worked for six months before it broke down and because it was only on a six-month guarantee we weren't able to take it back. We are still paying off the loan a year later.'

Switching a loan and consolidation loans You can switch your loan, but it's normally very expensive. If you are up to your eyeballs trying to balance credit cards you may be able to take out a consolidation loan. This allows you to pay off everything, swapping lots of payments for one monthly one.

Consolidation loans are not always the best answer. Although they may look cheaper, and more manageable, they may be more expensive in the long term. A consolidation loan may take longer to pay off, so, while you are paying off only £100 a month, you may end up doing so over a longer period of time, and that may mean more interest in the long run.

If you are having problems paying off your loan or credit card, speak to your loan or credit-card company first. They may be able to reduce or even freeze your interest. Just because you are paying off only one loan per month, it doesn't mean you are paying less in interest.

What you should look out for The APR. This is really the only thing you need to consider with a loan. A personal loan APR is slightly different from the APR on credit cards, store cards and overdrafts. The APR takes into account

£   the interest you must pay
£   any other charges you must pay – for example, an arrangement fee or the cost of payment insurance
£   when and how often you pay the interest and charges

You do not need to know how to work out an APR. The important thing is that APRs allow you to compare one loan with another and with credit cards and overdrafts too. A loan with a lower APR is cheaper than a loan with a higher APR.

Loans are good for ...

£   very large purchases that would be way too expensive to put on a credit card

£   when you really need to spread your money (this is especially true if you've just bought a home and you need to start furnishing it)

£   when you may need to bring all your debts together into a manageable amount

Not so good for ...

£   Frivolous purchases: you shouldn't be taking out loans to pay for new clothes or to pay off friends and family to whom you owe cash

And there are other ways of borrowing ...

CATALOGUES

Most of the well-known catalogues offer a form of credit that can be extremely sexy if you want to buy an autumn wardrobe in the middle of summer. But buying from a catalogue still means spending your own money.

'I love the Next catalogue because it comes out in July, just when you are getting really tired of the summer wardrobe,' says Mandy. 'So I quite often end up ordering about a thousand pounds' worth of bits, not just for me but my boyfriend, too. Some of it I return, but I nearly always end up keeping at least seven hundred pounds of it. Then of course when the collections come into the high street and designer stores I end up buying those, too. The reason I probably whack it all on my catalogue bill is because I can pay it over three months. Trouble is, I can't seem to get it through to myself that it's still money. It just doesn't seem like it.'

'My Freeman's bill is always huge,' says Tim. 'I probably wouldn't admit to my mates that I bought clothes from there. But I do.'

It seems there are a lot of closet catalogue shoppers around. Buying from a book can save us from the frantic almost druglike trance induced by shopping. Sitting in the comfort of your own home may allow you to be more rational and sensible about your purchases. But if you hit the shops as well you could be setting yourself up for a fall.

CREDIT CHECKS

Before you get a personal loan, a credit card or a store card, your financial history will be checked to ascertain whether you are a sure bet. Usually, this involves:

A CREDIT REFERENCE AGENCY – NO HIDING

Credit-reference agencies are companies that banks, credit cards and other financial companies use to check the credit history of a potential customer. A credit-reference agency – there are several in the UK – keeps records of every financial mistake we make, including defaults on a loan, or a credit card that's been run up out of control. However, they also keep a record of how good we have been as well. The file on you is publicly available information, such as your address and whether you have any county court judgments (CCJs) against you (these are court orders to repay your debts – see **Debt: The Good the Bad and the Ugly**). It also includes information about other loans you already have and whether you have kept up the payments on those. You have the right to check your credit file – the Office of Fair Trading website tells you how to do this (see below for the website address).

CREDIT SCORING

This is a system banks use to work out how much of a risk you are. They will ask you questions about your job, how long you have lived where you now live, how much you earn, whether you have a bank account and whether you have another loan or credit cards. You get a mark for each answer and these are totted up to determine your credit score. If you are to succeed in obtaining a card or loan, your score will have to be above a certain figure. The company will not tell you how its scoring system works or what you scored. If the provider thinks you are a bad risk – in other words, there's a chance you might not keep up repayments – you might be given a loan or card but with a low credit limit; sometimes you may be refused altogether.

BORROWING FROM FAMILY AND FRIENDS

Owing money to your family or mates may be cheap – I bet they don't charge the same rate of interest as a bank – but what you save on interest rates you end up paying in emotional credit points. Often this kind of debt is unavoidable, such as when you buy your first house, but think twice before you accept.

'I lent my sister two thousand pounds when she got into some serious financial trouble,' says Helen. 'About a year passed and she never offered to pay it back. Then, the next thing I knew my mum had rung me to tell me my sister was buying a house in Ireland, where my family live. Well, I was livid. I mean, I was living in London and couldn't even afford to buy my own home. What was she doing with my cash? I still hold it against her. And I still keep wondering whether she'll ever pay it back or not!'

Peter, aged 22, says, 'My brother gave me just over a thousand pounds to help me out when I bought my first home. Then, five years later, when we were out celebrating my mum's birthday over dinner, he told me he was having problems paying his mortgage, and did I have the thousand pounds? Of course I didn't but I didn't know what to do. I think the issue was that he had nowhere else to turn. I felt so bad because he'd helped me out when I needed it. Now I'm trying to lend him what cash I do have.'

YOUR OPTIONS

So the above are some options, but which one is best for you? Seeing through the fog that surrounds borrowing does not require a degree in astrophysics. What it does require is a far tougher call than that: a bit of self-awareness. Be honest with yourself, and you may just save some cash. First things first – how are you paid?

As regular as clockwork If you are paid regularly and are fairly organised with your cash, you have the wondrous luxury of being able to get your hands on practically all types of credit. Banks will love you because, with a regular income, you'll be able to afford monthly repayments.

What you should be looking for

Loans for larger purchases, because the interest works out lower than that on a credit card paid over the same period of time.

Credit cards as long as you are able to keep tabs on how much you owe. These are great for holidays, stereos and other things that can be split between a couple of months.

Overdraft as the cheapest way of borrowing money over the long term, as long as you've arranged it with your bank first.

Store cards too are OK, although remember that they do have higher interest rates than credit cards.

I get paid, but it sure isn't regular If you have nothing for ages and then it all comes in a rush, you'll have more difficulty obtaining credit. Multimillionaires may find their banks more than willing to sub them, but with mere mortals who are working on a freelance or subcontracting basis it can be a bit tricky.

What you should be looking for

Loans – although you should go easy on how much you borrow: overextending yourself with an expensive loan could give you a nasty financial hangover.

Overdraft is a cheaper way of borrowing than a loan, if you need to be careful on everyday expenses.

Credit cards and **store cards** – you can go for these, but remember that if you can't make the minimum repayment you'd still be best sticking to a loan.

Now ask yourself: What's my spending style?

You love splashing out Then you'll probably already have an eclectic mix of credit and store cards on the go. If you're paid regularly then that's no hassle; and if you choose to pay by direct debit, well, even better, because often you'll get a discount on your total balance for being so good. If you're one of the financially incontinent who spend, spend, spend, then you may be better off looking for a low-rate credit card (see 'Credit-card whoring'), and switching from it when the preferential interest rate expires. Overdrafts are another option.

You're careful but love luxury Then, so long as you're not up to your eyeballs in red ink, you can take out all types of credit.

You save and save and save and then some ... Your prudence would put Chancellor Gordon Brown to shame. You're probably best skipping this chapter and going on to the savings section.

CHANGING YOUR BANK ACCOUNT

This is a great option for those who simply have to have an overdraft. There are so many new Internet-based banks offering cheaper rates of interest that you'd be crazy not to shop around for a better deal; and there are also lots of current accounts that now pay out decent amounts of interest on accounts that are in credit. And it's not a hassle to swap all your standing orders and direct debits, either: in 2001 an automated system to swap customer information between banks increased the ease of moving accounts, and you don't have to pay an extra penny.

WHY CHANGE MY ACCOUNT?

£ You can get cheaper interest on what you borrow (your overdraft).

£ You may get more interest when you are in credit.

£ You may even be able to get a no-interest/cheap-interest deal.

£ You may be able to take advantage of extras such as life insurance and holiday insurance.

£ You are unhappy with the service you get.

With the advent of Internet banking, banks are becoming more shrewd than ever – there are accounts that allow you to offset any savings you may have against your overdraft, for instance. So, if you've got savings with the bank you've got an overdraft with, you may be able to get yourself a cheaper overdraft by sacrificing a higher rate on your savings. This may mean taking a cut in your savings interest rate, to save money repaying your debts.

HOW TO SWITCH

The bank you are switching to will normally take care of your direct debits, standing orders and regular bill payments. Some will even take care of any outstanding cheque payments due from your old account.

Will I be charged? No, you shouldn't be, but, if you are, chances are it will be by your 'old' bank, which may be reluctant to let a customer go. The new bank may compensate for any expenses incurred, so check when you swap.

How long will it take? Swap your account to an Internet-based bank and it could take just a few days. If your credit rating is good, that is.

What if I'm really not happy with my bank? The Banking Ombudsman can settle any queries you have. The numbers you need are listed in **Resources** at the end of the book.

One more not-so-little thing Before embarking on the next part of the path to financial enlightenment, there's something else you should consider: is your spending out of control? Having lots of credit at your fingertips can be absolute nirvana, but it can be an absolute nightmare, too, if you are starting to feel as if you are treading water. For ease, this chapter assumes that you haven't got into debt but that you are a bit worried about your financial habits.

Here are some early-warning signs you might want to heed:

- £   I often have next to no cash at the end of the month.
- £   I'm having to borrow money from my family and friends.
- £   I find that I'm waking up at 3 a.m. worried about money, and how I'm going to pay off my credit-card bill.
- £   I can't talk about money to my friends, family or partner.
- £   I try to avoid opening my bank statements, although I do open them.
- £   I've got loads of store cards, not all maxed out, but I keep fantasising as to what I'm going to buy with them.
- £   I'm starting to think about running away!

The benefits of retail therapy If you think watching your money is all doom and gloom and taking the fun out of spending your hard-earned cash, take heed of one or two benefits of what has come to be called 'retail therapy'.

- £   spending cash and buying things you need and want is a form of self-love (just remember that getting badly into debt isn't)
- £   spending money on your family and friends may be a superficial way of telling them how much you care, but it will also make them feel wonderful

SPENDING YOUR OWN MONEY – WAYS TO MAKE IT GO FURTHER

SPENDING RIGHT

If you are wanting to cut back on some spending, to save or make way for other purchases there are some really simple rules.

- £   Don't go to the supermarket when you are hungry.
- £   Don't shop for clothes or makeup when you are feeling fat/unhappy/unloved – desperation is never a good frame of mind to be in.
- £   Don't buy at first glance: there's no such thing as love at first sight when it comes to an item of designer gear. If it's a real love affair, you can wait a few days or weeks.
- £   If the thing you want sells out, don't become disheartened: there is always, always something else bigger, better and more sexy to buy.
- £   Try to buy fruit and vegetables from your local market stall, not the supermarket: you can always save the money you haven't spent to splash out with.
- £   Make friends with your local 'all-for-a-pound' store.
- £   Buy a season ticket if you travel by train.
- £   Learn to cycle if you travel by car.
- £   If you want to get fit and can't afford the gym, get yourself to a local park and run.

HOLIDAYS

- £   Book on the Internet; and, if you can leave it to the last minute, do: chances are your holiday will be even cheaper.
- £   When you are changing holiday cash, go somewhere that doesn't charge commission.
- £   Take your credit card on holiday with you for emergencies.
- £   If you travel a lot, invest in an annual holiday-insurance policy, rather than having to pay each time you go.
- £   Remember: children travel more cheaply, so never pay full price for them.

INDULGENCES

If you want to take up an expensive sport, borrow the gear until you're sure you are into it; then, if you love it, by all means splash out.

SOD DESIGNER LABELS

Learn to love the cheapie shops – designer gear is not everything. Be proud of *not* wearing designer gear (ignore the fact that just about everyone else is wearing it) – that way you'll be individual and stylish. Or, if you can hack it, share clothes with your mates.

FURNISH YOUR HOME

You don't have to buy out Heals or Habitat to have a home that comes out of the pages of *Elle Decoration*. Katie managed to decorate her home by looking closer to home. 'Second-hand furniture stores can be great places,' she says. 'My mother managed to kit my sister out with a cot, baby carrier and dressing table from a nearly-new shop in Bishop's Stortford. If you can get to the country you can actually buy unusual or reconditioned furniture.'

CLOTHES

If you've got some half-decent gear, take it to a dress agency, then put the cash you make into a savings account. Baby clothes are expensive, but do make excellent hand-me-downs. Even blokes' clothes can come cheap, as one enterprising young man – Zack, aged 35 – points out. 'When I moved out of London to downsize my life for that of a country gardener/florist,' he says, 'I had a clothes party, where I sold all my Hugo Boss and Dolce & Gabbana suits along with some of my ties and shirts. I made some cash and my mates got some designer things on the cheap.'

MANAGING YOUR BANK ACCOUNT(S)

Most of us keep our cash in a bank account with very little idea of how they actually work. Well be a dunce no longer. Here's our guide to bank accounts.

CURRENT ACCOUNTS

Current accounts let you go overdrawn, unlike savings accounts or individual savings accounts (ISAs – see **Saving**). But, like savings accounts, they do pay interest if you are in credit. The rate of interest you get differs wildly from bank to bank, and the Internet-based banks often pay better rates than the high street ones because they have fewer overheads than branches do, with their need for buildings and staff.

What kind of current account you go for will depend on how you manage your account.

'During my student days my account was always overdrawn, so, while I was at college, I went for an account that didn't charge me much on my overdraft,' says John. 'Then, when I finally paid it all off, I worked out that I would be better off switching to an account that paid more interest on my balance.'

CURRENT ACCOUNTS AND BANKS

Once upon a time it used to be only banks that offered us current accounts. Now building societies are in on the act, as are many Internet companies. But not just anyone can set up as a bank: all UK companies that offer current accounts have been given a licence to operate by the Bank of England, so the Bank of England is responsible if things go wrong.

However, some current accounts that are run on the Internet are not run by UK banks: some are run by US and European banks, and that's when things get complicated. You can check by going into the bank's site and clicking on contact details.

MUTUAL ADMIRATION

Some current accounts pay good rates of interest if you are in credit, and also have cheap overdrafts. These accounts tend, though not always, to be run by mutual societies. A bank is not a mutual society because it is owned by shareholders. Examples of mutual companies include building societies and co-operatives. The Co-operative Bank and Nationwide are two well-known mutuals. In theory, they are owned by their customers, known as policyholders.

WHAT YOU GET WITH A CURRENT ACCOUNT

When you open your account you'll normally be given a cash card that triples as a debit card and a cheque-guarantee card. Most bank cards use Visa, Switch, Delta or Electron technology; sometimes they may have a combination of several. What this means is that you can use a cash machine displaying these signs, or pay with your card in a shop that has the machines that use the Switch or Visa technology.

ANOTHER KIND OF CURRENT ACCOUNT

You can have two current accounts but, if you are in credit, it will make more sense to have just the one. If you have a partner, and you share bills, you may want to open a current account especially for bills and other household expenses.

There are current accounts that don't let you get overdrawn, these tend to come with a cash card but no cheque book and no overdraft facility. These accounts are great for managing day-to-day finances, but not if you often find yourself running low on cash at the end of the month.

RULES FOR GOOD BANKING

Before we get carried away, here are some rules for running your current account as safely as possible.

Internet security If you have an Internet account, always check that the site you are using displays a padlock, usually at the bottom right of your browser. This means your details are secure and can be accessed only by you and the bank.

At the cash machine When using a cash machine try to make sure no one else can see your PIN (your *personal identification number*, which the bank gives you when you get your card). If someone tries to distract you while you are withdrawing your money, ignore them.

Keep it separate Keep your cheque card separate from your cheque book. Keep your cards in a safe place, and keep a written note of your card numbers in case you do lose them or they are stolen.

PAYING BILLS

You can go the old-fashioned route, and use a cheque, but it's far better to pay by direct debit or standing order.

Direct debits When you sign a direct-debit agreement, you are giving the company you pay bills to the power to take whatever they like from your current account. It's not that frightening, though: under a direct-debit agreement they have to let you know a few weeks in advance what they will be deducting from your bank account. If you do need to cancel a direct debit you may need to get permission from the company you are paying the bill to, though not always.

Standing orders A standing order is a set, unchanging amount agreed to by you. Both direct debits and standing orders take about three days to go from your bank account to your bill company. A standing order can be cancelled by you alone.

Bill payments If you are still concerned about paying some bills this way you can set up a bill-payment facility, which holds all the bank details of the company you are paying. All you have to do is ring your bank up and tell them how much your bill is for, and they do the rest. You can set up a bill-payment facility on your cash card – this allows you to pay bills at cash machines if you haven't got time to go to your bank.

PAYING MONEY IN

You can get your salary paid direct to your account so that it's available the same day. In fact, most companies now pay their employees by a system known as BACS (which stands for *Bankers Automated Clearing System*). You can pay cheques in by post, or even through a cash machine – some let you deposit the money via an envelope. Both of these methods take a few days, though, so if you need to deposit the money in a hurry then it would be better to go to a branch of your bank. Paying into an Internet account can normally be done by post or through your local post office. Never send cash by post – it will probably go missing.

WHEN YOU CAN GET AT YOUR MONEY

If you get your salary paid direct into your account you should be able to get at it straightaway. If you are paying cash in you'll also be able to get it there and then. Cheques and bankers' drafts may take longer, depending on what kind of current account you have. Some accounts will let you have the money two days later, while others may take longer. Some banks offer an emergency cheque-clearing service, but you'll probably have to pay a fee for this.

CHEQUES AND DEBIT CARDS

If you pay by cheque you will need to show your cheque-guarantee card. This lets the person you are paying know that you are who you say you are and that you have enough money in your current account to pay them. If you are paying by post you won't need to send your card with your cheque. Cheques can take a while to clear – this is when they are paid out from your account. Debit cards are a much better way of paying if you are buying face to face, or even by phone, because the money will come out of your current account the same day, making it easier for you to manage your finances.

TRANSFERRING MONEY BETWEEN ACCOUNTS

If you are trying to pay off an overdraft or put savings away and you have your accounts all within the same bank, you should be able to transfer them easily from one to another. If you have a savings account with another bank or building society, use a standing order instead.

MONEY ABROAD

There was a time when people just took traveller's cheques with them on holiday. Even that wasn't enough for Garry. 'We were in Thailand, on Ko Phi Phi, the island that they based the film *The*

Beach on,' he says, 'and I'd run out of cash. This was in 1985 and none of the shops – and there weren't that many – took traveller's cheques. Thank God my travelling partner Julia had some cash on her: we'd have starved otherwise.'

Now one of the safest ways to carry money abroad is probably your debit card. If you are going on holiday to Europe you can use practically any cash machine. But it can still be an expensive business, as Julia found out last year. 'I'd kept withdrawing cash like you do in the UK, the odd twenty euros here and there. When I got back each withdrawal had cost me £1.50. I'd have been much better off taking large sums out of my account instead.'

CASH ABROAD: KEY POINTS

£   **Some travel agents and banks offer commission-free traveller's cheques.**

£   **Taking your credit card abroad is a good insurance policy in case you are stuck for cash.**

£   **In Europe you can use your current account's debit card to withdraw cash; Solo, Switch, Visa, Electron, Delta are accepted by nearly all European banks and some US ones, too.**

Of course, cash can be covered on a holiday-insurance policy and traveller's cheques can be replaced. Having access to cash in several different forms is your best bet.

FINDING OUT WHAT'S ON YOUR CREDIT RECORD

You are entitled to find out what information credit agencies hold on you by contacting them direct. Often the agency will want you to send a cheque – £2 or so – along with a form detailing your addresses for the last six years. There are two main credit agencies used by banks and building societies, and they tend to vary. Your best bet is to find out from your bank which agency they use – they'll normally tell you when they refuse you credit.

CHECKING YOUR CREDIT RATING

If you want to know more about your rights or you think you've been wrongly blacklisted by a credit agency, you should contact your local Citizens' Advice Bureau or trading-standards authority, which may have a money advice centre to deal with financial problems. You can get the number from your phone book.

You can also get lots of information from the Office of Fair Trading – the details are at the end of **Debt: The Good the Bad and the Ugly**, with some other useful contact information.

TO ALL SPENDERS

Please, please, please, also remember that banks and borrowers are covered under law, so, if you do decide to borrow from a more obscure company, such as one that does its business only via the Internet, check its financial credentials first. This is very important when dealing with a company you, your friends and family have not heard of.

It's always a good idea to make sure you are actually borrowing from a registered, and above-board, organisation. Any time you borrow you should be presented with, and asked to sign, a *consumer credit agreement* – this protects you as much as the company you are borrowing from. And make time to read the small print – this will include the things we have already mentioned: penalty charges for missed repayments or charges for early repayment. It will also outline your rights as a borrower under the Consumer Credit Act 1974.

And, if you feel a lender has treated you unfairly, get in touch with your local trading-standards office, or better still, read **Debt: The Good the Bad and the Ugly**.

2 DEBT: THE GOOD THE BAD AND THE UGLY

Spending money is great while you've got it, isn't it? And, as with a lot of the things in life that you love, there is always the downside of overindulgence: one spending expedition can lead to a financial hangover lasting years.

Then there are some, even the careful ones, who find a sudden lack of finances comes and bites them on the bum when they least expect it to. But, no matter how you got it, you *can* cope with that twenty-first-century essential, debt.

'I so desperately wanted my independence,' says 44-year-old Peter. 'I was seventeen and I lived on a farm in the middle of nowhere. The nearest bus stop was two miles away and the nearest town was six miles away. So I got a job as a sheet-metal worker and used that to get me a loan so I could buy myself a motorbike. Since then I've spent the rest of my life in debt, living from one pay day to the next, but I don't regret for one minute buying that bike. Even out of all the things I've bought since, I'll always remember that motorbike. It was one of the most fabulous things I ever had.'

Peter started with good intentions: he knew the bike would help him change his life, but he couldn't afford it. So he used the 'generosity' of his bank to finance his dream of independence.

This is a long way down the retail evolutionary scale – when our grandparents wanted something they had to save up for it.

'I remember the most fantastic dress in Fenwick, a great department store in Bond Street,' says Ella, a wistful sixty-year-old. 'I spent six months saving up for it. I used to go in each week with my pay packet and pay a little bit more towards it. When I got that dress it was the best feeling, but I still can't help but feel a bit envious when I see my daughter go out and splash hundreds of pounds on a designer dress. She simply puts her credit card on the counter and it's hers. I often wonder if she really appreciates just how lucky she is.'

That may sound like anathema to many of us: 'Save up for something? You've got to be kidding!' That's probably why so many of us are wedded to debt: we have to have everything now, and we know we can.

If you got into debt in the 1940s, 1950s or even 1960s you'd either been misbehaving or had a generous bank manager. The truth is that most of us slow down only when we're forced to, when our debts get to such an unmanageable level that we end up being forced to take stock of our spending habits – as Mike had to. 'I've spent most of my twenties paying off one debt only to get another, with the result that I now owe over twenty thousand pounds on credit cards, loans, shop cards, you name it,' he says. 'I didn't go to university, so, unlike most of my mates, I've always been earning. It started with a credit card, something I took out for my first job, and just spiralled from there. I was sensible and got a mortgage but that was just the start of it. I only wanted the best furniture for my pad, so I ended up getting every kind of store and credit card going, ending up with twenty thousand pounds – my mortgage was sixty thousand.

'I took out loans to pay off the credit cards, only to get another credit card. It got pretty scary and I ended up remortgaging on my house to pay off debts.

'In the end I knew that it wasn't the fact that I wasn't earning enough, just that I basically loved spending money. There's nothing like that high you get when you buy something on a whim. In fact it can even seem a bit of a high when you know you don't really have the money. It's a kind of rebellion because I've always been so good – getting a sensible job, giving my mum and dad decent housekeeping when I lived at home.'

But how to know when to throw in the towel when it comes to debts? Here's a colour-coded guide.

GREEN FOR GO: YOUR DEBTS ARE MANAGEABLE

£   Less than a third of your monthly pay goes on paying off debts, or a quarter if you don't have a mortgage.

£   You have only one credit card, and you manage to pay a large chunk of it off each month. Sometimes you may not even owe any cash on it at all.

£   You've always got money to spare at the end of the month, even if it's only £20.

£   You've got some kind of long-term savings goal and you manage to put cash by for it – even only a small amount – each month.

AMBER: GO EASY

£   You keep taking out credit cards to pay other ones off.

£   Some months you run out of money.

£   You often have to borrow cash from friends and family.

£   You often reach the limit of your overdraft.

£   You are a sporadic saver, and sometimes you end up dipping into your savings.

£   You have a long-term savings plan only when you're drunk, but you forget about it in the morning.

RED: STOP – YOUR DEBTS ARE NOT UNDER CONTROL

£   You can't open bank statements, because you're too scared to look.

£   You lie to your partner about how much you earn/owe.

£   You're having to put essentials on your credit card, even though you earn more than £40,000 a year and you received a big bonus at Christmas.

£   You've got a string of store cards, credit cards and loans and they're all up to their limit.

£   You can't remember what cash looks like – in fact, you tried to eat the last coin you saw because you thought it was made of chocolate.

SYMPTOMS OF SERIOUS DEBT

A POOR OR NONEXISTENT CREDIT RATING

This means that there's a big black mark somewhere being held against you that will affect your ability to take out more credit. This could be a blessing in disguise if you are already pushing things to the limit. But sometimes you can get yourself a minus credit point simply by missing a loan repayment, or moving home and forgetting you owe a catalogue £10. Book clubs will often register if you forget to pay them £5.

LOSING AT LEAST ONE FRIENDSHIP BECAUSE YOU OWE THEM MONEY

On a scale of one to ten, in the book of how not to run up debts this can rate on an eight. Friendships are more important than cash and no good friend is worth losing over money. 'Neither a borrower nor a lender be' unless you go into business or buy a house together, in which case your finances are entwined together, anyway. Even then proceed with caution.

A COUNTY COURT JUDGMENT

A CCJ against you means you've got yourself into some serious financial trouble. The company you owe money to has gone to a civil court (county court – hence the name) to get its cash back. The CCJ will put you under a legal obligation to repay a certain amount back, or risk having your possessions seized.

People get county court judgments for lots of reasons: you may move and owe a phone company for a bill you've completely forgotten, or you may have run up a huge catalogue or credit-card bill that you can no longer afford to pay back.

Warning Once you've got a CCJ it will be mentioned on your credit-agency file until you've paid off what you owe. Even when you do pay it back, it doesn't mean all mention of it will be wiped out. CCJs can stop you obtaining credit, so it's important that you try to avoid getting them in the first place, as CCJ victim, Imogen, points out. 'My mum was made homeless; she had a business but ended up owing water rates. Of course, because I was down on the electoral roll as living with her when she started to owe money I was implicated too. When all the papers started coming through I didn't think to get her to take my name off. Then, when I went to take out a mortgage, guess what: I'd got a CCJ against my name. It took a lot of hassle to get it wiped off: my mum had to write to loads of people and I even had to contact the office of trading standards a couple of times because even after all that effort the damn thing kept showing up on my credit file.'

And here's another less ominous tale from a 23-year-old student, Sally. 'I owed a catalogue fifty pounds but, because I moved, it completely and utterly slipped my mind. Next thing I knew they'd tracked me down with a county court judgment – for *seventy* pounds, to include the costs I owed them to boot. But I was told that, as long as I paid the CCJ off within a few weeks, it would not be held on my credit file. Of course I cleared it straightaway. The following year I managed to get a mortgage and a credit card, with no problems.'

The good thing about a CCJ is that the person you owe money to will stop adding interest once it's registered, and the court will set repayments at an amount you can afford.

As long as you keep up your repayments the creditor is not allowed to use any other ways of clawing their money back, such as the use of bailiffs.

ATTACHMENT-OF-EARNINGS ORDERS

An attachment-of-earnings order means that you failed to make efforts to repay your debts – normally following a county court judgment – so, instead, the company you owe the money to has applied for a court order to take the money straight out of your wages. You will normally have to give the court details of your salary and they set your repayments at an affordable rate.

THE BAILIFFS

The idea of men wearing black coats carrying clipboards and cleaning you out of house and home to pay off a string of debts is not that passé. Bailiffs are still used to recoup costs, but as a last resort. Bailiffs are sent in when you default on a CCJ repayment or fail to keep up an attachment-of-earnings agreement.

Bailiffs are not the same as debt collectors, who are not allowed to take any action against you – unlike bailiffs, they cannot force you to hand over cash or your prized possessions. If you do not let bailiffs in, they cannot take what is known as 'walking possession' of your things, but they can take things not inside the house, such as a car. Bailiffs do not tend to take essential household items, so they may take a stereo but not a cooker.

GOOD DEBTS TO HAVE

There are still some kinds of debt, see **Spending It**, that it's OK to have. A mortgage, for example, is normally seen as a good debt because you're paying off something that could end up making you money. Here are some more.

£ a manageable loan
£ a credit card that charges a reasonable amount of interest
£ a store card you use only for special occasions
£ an overdraft that you are paying off

And here are a few bad debts to have.

£ anything that you can no longer manage
£ money borrowed from a loan shark
£ those you have to take from a credit card in order to buy food
£ a consolidation loan that actually works out more expensive than your debts would individually

GETTING TO GRIPS WITH YOUR DEBT

Ridding yourself of debts means being honest. If your spending habits are getting out of control, the worst thing you can do is beat yourself up about it. That will make you feel worse and you may feel more scared to confront it. So here's what to do.

£ Set aside a weekend when you know you've got no commitments, and therefore no excuses not to sort yourself out.
£ Promise yourself that, when you've sorted yourself out, you'll treat yourself to something really special.
£ If you can invite a good friend over or share all of this with your partner, do so – it will really help.
£ Then take out all your bank statements, credit-card slips and red bills and have a really good look at where all your money goes and when.
£ Make a list in a notebook of the things you buy, putting them under different headings. You may find out that you spend less on clothes and more on coffee than you think.

THEN WHAT?

£ If you are having real problems, then you'll need to contact your credit-card company or bank and tell them that you are.
£ If you're just about managing for the next week, live on cash only – don't take your credit cards anywhere. See how you get on. Do you get panicky, for instance (in which case, you should ring the National Debtline), or do you feel liberated?

THE GOOD THING ABOUT DEBT

Owing money can turn you sick with worry but it can also help make you more aware of the value of cold, hard cash. People who've spent years building up their credit-card debt can be more resourceful when they do get a few quid. Chances are that, if you're in debt, you'll probably be more resourceful with the cash you do spend on food. If you're willing to learn, being in debt could turn you into a richer person.

Nikki left university with a £700 overdraft. Luckily, she just missed out on the student-loan era. One £12,000-a-year job and two years later, she had a £3,000 loan, £3,000 on credit cards and a £1,000 overdraft.

'When my boyfriend and friends asked me where all the money had gone – I never seemed to have spare cash for presents and meals out – I was at a complete loss. I hadn't amassed a wardrobe of expensive clothes; I hadn't spent every night boozing in the wine bar; and I hadn't even left home.

'I stopped looking at my bank statements. To make matters worse, the business my parents owned went under and we were made homeless. Then I was offered a place on a postgraduate journalism course, which would cost three thousand pounds. I had to do the course. My parents scraped enough money to rent somewhere for the family. But I was forced to make some major changes in my life. My first journalism job paid me just seven thousand a year, and by this stage I owed nearly twelve thousand.

'It has taken me nearly ten years to pay it all back, and because I've had to budget so much I've learned how to make a little bit of cash go a long way.'

BAD THINGS ABOUT DEBT

Nikki's story above is certainly salutary, but it illustrates that debt can have a positive effect on your attitude, even if it's a hard slog getting there. Here, though, are some definitely *bad* things about debt.

£   It makes you sick with worry: ever had your appetite ruined by a red bill?

- £ It stops you enjoying life: you can't go on that skiing holiday/buy your dream home.
- £ It ruins relationships: 'Please may I borrow some cash?'
- £ It turns you into a liar: 'It only cost thirty pounds.' (Three hundred, more like!)

STUDENT DEBT

Anyone under the age of thirty who's studied has had to live with debt. A student survey carried out by Barclays Bank showed that the average amount owed by students went up to £6,228 per year of study in 2002, compared with £5,961 the year before.

If you have just graduated or are about to, you do not have to be a maths whiz to solve the quandary: exactly how quickly should you be paying off your debts? If you are lucky enough to get a lump sum, should you use it to pay off your debts, or should you invest it? If you're clever, you can do both.

PAYING YOUR WAY

Since 1998 students have had to pay something towards the cost of their tuition fees – except Scottish students studying in Scotland. Finding that extra £3,000 to £5,000 is going to put more pressure on your finances. Students are no longer able to get grants, so most of those wanting to go into further or higher education have to take out a loan through the Student Loans Scheme or rely on their parents.

There are other ways you can save cash while at university or college.

- £ Student railcards and coach cards give you a reduction on travel costs. You can get these however old you are, so long as you are in full-time education (although you need to show proof that you are on a course).
- £ In most cases students are exempt from paying council tax. There are exceptions, in which case you may get a discount. Check with your benefits office.
- £ Students can usually get cheaper insurance.
- £ You can pool your food bills with other students.
- £ Try sharing taxis and car journeys to campus.

STUDENT LOANS: HOW MUCH DO I PAY BACK?

College leavers who started their course after September 1998 start their loan repayments once they earn £10,000 or over, before tax.

Once you hit that salary, your repayments will be made via your National Insurance contributions, or through self-assessment if your are self-employed. A total of 9 per cent of your monthly salary is automatically deducted to pay off the loan, which has an interest rate set at inflation, so it is cheaper than most normal loans.

Those still on courses that began before September 1998 do not have to start repaying their loans until their monthly salary is more than £1,644 – that's £19,000 before they get taxed.

Remember that if you lose your job you are exempt from repaying the loan.

LOANS AND MORTGAGES WHILE YOU ARE A STUDENT

Some financial advisers see no reason why a graduate should not take out a mortgage, as long as they can cope with their repayments – so shop around.

If you've got a good credit record then you will have no problem taking out a mortgage. However, it is a very good idea to bring down your debts to a manageable level. In some cases, especially outside London, it's actually cheaper to pay a mortgage than pay out on rent.

SAVING MONEY AFTER GRADUATION

£   Stay at home for a few months after university to save on rent.
£   Get a local job that means you don't have to shell out for travel.
£   Try to eat in as much as you can; invite friends round.
£   If you travel, do it cheaply. If you are under 26 you'll still be allowed to use your Young Person's Railcard.
£   Switch your bank account to one that gives you a free overdraft.
£   Check with your bank about postgraduate loan deals that offer cheaper rates of interest than standard loans.

Pay off your most expensive debts first, after you've worked out what deals your bank may have for you as a new graduate.

Start with your overdraft, then think about transferring your credit card balance to a card paying a transfer rate of zero per cent (turn back to **Spending It**, for details on credit cards).

Joanne, a graduate of City University in London, used the knowledge gleaned from her four-year business-management degree to get herself on the straight and narrow. 'I paid off the balance of my credit card during the interest-free period, but I didn't buy anything else with it. That gave me a bit of breathing space – it was really in effect an interest-free loan.

'I also deferred my student loan as long as I could because it was set at such a low rate of interest. I waited till my overdraft was clear before I started paying it off.'

LOANS – A WARNING

Cash-strapped you may be, but taking out a loan may not be the best idea. You should really be limiting your expenses. One of the most disappointing things about graduating can be that the money you do earn will have to be used to pay back debts.

LOSING YOUR JOB

Of the many ways of getting into debt losing your job is the most common. There are a couple of ways you can find yourself out of work.

- £ Being sacked. This is a different kettle of fish from simply being out of a job that no longer exists. If your firm has decided that you are no longer capable of doing your job, or you have acted dishonestly, then you will be lucky to get any kind of cash. If you feel you have been unfairly dismissed then contact your nearest Citizens' Advice Bureau or your union.
- £ Being made redundant. Through no fault of your own the company you are working for decides that your services, skills and brilliant all-roundedness are suddenly surplus to requirements. When you are made redundant and the company you are working for is still in business, you may get a lump sum of cash to cushion the loss of your job.

REDUNDANCY EXPLAINED

What am I entitled to? It depends on your notice period, so the longer your notice period the more you'll usually get. That's why it pays to make sure your notice period is the maximum possible: notice periods generally vary between one week and three months – and can be even higher. Your redundancy payment can be given as a lump sum or monthly, like a salary.

Do I get anything else? There may be outstanding holiday entitlement, but this will be taxed, even if your redundancy payment isn't. If you've been working for your firm for less than two years, you normally get just your notice period, although some firms do in some circumstances pay out more. Legally, though, once you've been working (full time or part time) for a firm for more than two years, you are entitled to one week's pay for every year of service.

If you are over 41 and under 64, this goes up to one and a half weeks' pay. But for every month over the age of 64 you start to lose one-twelfth of that, so if you are 64 and six months you'll get only half what you would have done the year before. Once you're over 65 you get nothing.

Bonuses and golden handshakes are not taxed as long as they are under £30,000. Share options and other benefits you leave with will be taxed according to your normal tax code. You may also even be entitled to take a refund of your pension contributions if you have been paying into a company scheme, although normally this happens only if you've been paying in for less than two years. If you've been paying in for more than two years, you may still be allowed to a refund – it depends on the rules of your pension scheme. If you are in a personal pension organised by your company – a group personal pension (see **Getting Old**) – then your pension fund will be frozen and you will not get your cash back until you retire.

So what's garden leave? This is when you are still paid a salary by your old company but you are allowed to look for other jobs in addition to, well, hanging out in the garden. This kind of redundancy will have some stipulations: you may not be allowed in the office, for instance, or be able to take up a post with a rival firm.

Carrie worked for a pharmaceutical firm that made some of its staff redundant. 'Scientists in our company were made redundant and given garden leave,' she explains. 'They weren't allowed in the office and they had to sign agreements stopping them from passing on secrets they'd learned while working for the firm. They did have use of their cars, though.'

Can I negotiate for more? At the moment this is a pretty tough call to make. It depends why you are being made redundant. If the firm you are working for is cash-strapped, asking for more may be impossible. If it has made you redundant and others are being promoted, then it may be worth going back and asking for more.

Giving yourself a redundancy comfort blanket If you're careful, there are other things you can do to keep the cash flowing if you lose your job.

Savings Unfashionable up to now, good old savings, such as a basic post office account, are about to come in handy. Lesley needed hers when she lost her job as a technical writer. 'I cannot stress to anyone how important it is that they have three months' worth of salary in some kind of instant-access account,' she counsels. 'I got made redundant and my partner was just starting to build up a business. We had a whacking great mortgage, all based on my fifty-K salary.

'The company I was working for was going under, big time, owing loads of cash to creditors all over the world. The employees only got a month's salary. The worst thing was, I was pregnant at the time. Luckily, Nigel, my husband, was able to get a job. It didn't pay a lot but it did keep the mortgage going and pay our food bill.'

Insurance Some people with lots of financial commitments, such as a mortgage or loan, take out accident, sickness and redundancy insurance. It is not cheap: the average policy requires you to pay a minimum £5 premium per month for every £100 worth of mortgage repayments, and you cannot take it out if you are self-employed or working part time. This kind of insurance will not pay out until three months after you are made redundant, although payment is normally backdated to the first mortgage repayment missed. Some policies pay out for two years while some pay out for only one.

You can also take out loan and credit-card protection, which pays out under similar circumstances.

Remember: these policies are an option, but you have to prove there was no whiff of redundancy when you took them out.

What do I do now? Even if you have got enough cash to cover your mortgage repayments, you should still let your bank or building society know.

There may be a period when things get tight, especially if it takes longer than you expect to get another job. It sounds pretty simple but you will need to budget. Unless you have a tidy sum put away in savings then you should keep your cash where you can get at it very easily. As soon as you start working again there may be a delay in when you get your month's salary, so bear that in mind.

DEBT FLASHPOINTS

There can be several of these: Christmas, birthdays, other expensive occasions. They happen to us all.

If your greatest Christmas wish is to have money to pay off your debts you may have to go easy when you start planning your festive splurge. There's nothing worse than spending the whole year, or even half a year, paying out for Christmas.

Look at why you spend so much. Even people who are normally really sensible – the sickening kind who pay their bills on time and never get overdrawn – are tempted to spend, spend, spend. Psychologists who have looked into our spending habits say that it's seen as a sign of poverty and thoughtlessness if we don't spend much at Christmas. Which means we have an emotional need to prove ourselves by spending lots on decorations, clothes and food.

We also want other people to love us. There's also that temptation to judge our popularity by what other people buy us.

Louise, a clothes buyer for a big Leeds department store, hates Christmas for this reason: 'We [her friends from college days] have all known each other for five years, and since we've all been earning more and more money – not that many of us are rich – the Christmas-present buying has become more and more about who gets the best and most expensive present. I don't even want to buy them a present this year.'

SHOP, SHOP, SHOP?

It's not all down to us, of course: shops are always out to lure us into spending our money. They make their displays glisten with glitter and Christmas promise; they make their stores smell nicer; they even pipe sexy smells around the place, such as coffee, popcorn and freshly baked bread, in a blatant attempt to coax our credit cards and cash out of our purses and wallets. And of course many shops offer their own store cards now, with that tempting promise of being able to buy now and pay later.

DON'T BE A SPOILSPORT

Surely, telling us we can't spend at Christmas is a bit like telling a five-year-old that Santa doesn't exist.

'Moderation at this time of year is tough, but it can be done,' says Jacqui. She has worked out that sticking it on your card, or going over your already stretched overdraft limit, doesn't always work.

Jacqui, an only child, overspent last Christmas, and has ended up paying for it – literally. 'I lost my mother and father in the space of a couple of years and last year I just went mad, spending over three thousand pounds – most of that went on cards. I already had some debts, anyway. Basically, I wanted to make up for not having my family around, so I bought lots of my cousins expensive presents and my boyfriend ended up getting some fantastic things like an MP3 player. I've paid it all off but it took till July! This year I'm going to stick to a budget.'

WHEN IS IT TOO MUCH?

It's easy to try to resolve problems by buying presents. Christmas really is a time of coming together and the pressure is enormous. We think we can spend our way out of family arguments, and believe that if we buy the right present then everything really will be all right for the rest of the year. It's important to be aware of why we spend our money.

MANAGING YOUR MONEY AT CHRISTMAS

£ Take only cash with you when you shop. 'You immediately become aware of how much you are spending,' reckons Marianne, 'and, if you find that you're running out of cash quickly, you know that you are probably overdoing it on the cash front.'

£ Make a budget. 'Take a tip from your granny,' advises Marc, 'and make a list of exactly what you should and should not be buying: food, cards, decorations, presents and even how much you can spend on your Christmas outfits – and be realistic.'

£ Pay your bills. 'Set aside the money you really do need,' says Rob, 'such as mortgage or rent, gas or electricity bills, council tax and other loans you may have. Once you've paid these you'll know what you have left to spend.'

£ Recycle. 'You're not stingy if you use last year's Christmas cards as gift tags, and there's only so much tinsel you can buy after all,' claims Annalise.

Caroline has a novel idea of making December easier on the pocket, involving some bottles of wine and lots of friends. 'We make a point each year of having a couple of drunken evenings in when we invite mates round and make decorations using paper and old bits of card. We buy some glitter and glue it on to the cards. It reminds us of our schooldays.'

SAVING MONEY ON CHRISTMAS – ALL YEAR ROUND

£ Join a union. Good old-fashioned credit unions are becoming a fashionable and savvy way to budget for the festive season or other big occasions that require financial clout. Credit unions are savings schemes run by members. They allow you to borrow twice, or even three times, as much money as you've saved for a very low rate of interest. The best thing for you to do is contact the Association of British Credit Unions, which can explain the rules of setting up a union.

£ All year round. Save a little each month to allow for a Christmas blowout you can afford.

£ Shop around. Take the temptation to spend, spend, spend away by picking up copies of every shopping catalogue you can. Most shops do publish Christmas specials for you to browse at home. This will help you budget by giving you an idea of how much things cost and helping you track down must-have items without being distracted by all too persuasive shop assistants.

£ Shop on the Net. It can be the best way to grab a bargain. You can shop around and save the money you would have spent traipsing around the shops. Many things, such as books and homeware, are cheaper when bought on the Internet. 'My family live in New Zealand,' says Lisa, 'so ordering from the Internet is great for me. Their presents get delivered and they get them all wrapped up. But you should make sure that each site you buy from displays a padlock on the right-hand side of the browser page – this means it's secure enough to buy from.'

£ Have joint celebrations. Share the cost of Christmas parties and get together by offering to bring drink or different food courses. 'This year I've decided to have the whole family around for Christmas,' says Katherine. 'The difference is that we have had a baby and money is a bit tight, so my mum is making the dessert, my sister and her husband are bringing the turkey and all I have to do is provide the wine.'

WHEN IT'S NOT YOU WHO'S IN DEBT

Do you have a relative or friend who is having serious money problems, or who seems to be having trouble coping with cash?

'One of my relatives killed himself because he owed thousands of pounds,' says Barry, telling a cautionary tale. 'While I couldn't actually help him out, I know that I could at least have pointed out where he could have sought such advice without having to resort to the most desperate measure of all. He never talked about it.' Barry is still feeling guilty some ten years after that tragic suicide.

£ Talk to another person about it. Sharing your concerns with a friend or family member you and the other person have in common is a good idea. They might have noticed something, too.

£ Listen to the person who's having trouble. This is one of the most underrated social skills of all. You don't have to bombard them with questions about their saving or spending habits: just be there for them.

£ Drop subtle hints. It may not be just debt advice that you ought to be giving. There may be other reasons why they are in debt: they may have a gambling habit, or they may have taken out a dodgy loan. If that's the case, they may be able to get legal help (see the phone numbers at the end of the chapter).

WHEN YOU FEEL IT'S YOUR SPENDING THAT'S OUT OF CONTROL

IF YOU CAN'T SHARE A PROBLEM ...

If you want to speak to an impartial third person, then the National Debtline is a good place to start – see the end of the chapter for more numbers.

GIVE YOURSELF A BREAK

'My sister had always been fairly conservative with money, but when her boyfriend died she suddenly started coming home with loads of clothes, most of which were never worn,' says Louise. 'It only took a few months before she was admitting she had a problem. Thankfully, we were able to help her when the shock of losing Jack wore off and she was forced to confront her feelings. Problem is, she did have to do it while she was facing loads of debt.'

STOP AND THINK

This works better if you don't have any credit or cash cards on you – see the spending-junkie tale of John above. You need to make sure you have only enough available cash to spend on basics, such as food.

GIVE YOURSELF A TREAT BUDGET

This is so you don't feel like you are missing out. It doesn't have to be much: £10 a week to spend on coffee or sweets or chocolate may be enough.

WHEN TOO MUCH IS TOO MUCH

If you have taken out a loan and the company who lent you the money are now demanding what seems like an awful lot of interest, you may be able to get them to reduce it. The Consumer Credit Act gives the courts power to help people who – for whatever reason – have ended up borrowing at an extortionate rate. And sometimes the company who've lent the money can be ordered to repay unreasonable interest charges. You can get more information on this from the Office of Fair Trading.

LAST RESORT: BANKRUPTCY

Bankruptcy is serious. You can do it voluntarily or – and this is more likely to happen if you own a business that owes a lot of money – by a court order. You have to owe only £750 to be made bankrupt.

Being bankrupt means you may have to give up some possessions; and, if you have bought a home, you may have to give up that, too. You may also be prevented from having a bank account, getting a mortgage, borrowing money and a few more things besides. The Insolvency Service can help.

CAN I GET JAILED FOR BEING IN DEBT?

It's a frightening thought, but you needn't get too worried. There are only so many circumstances that can lead to jail: for instance, if ...

- £ **you haven't paid fines**
- £ **you haven't paid your council tax**
- £ **you haven't paid maintenance to a husband/wife or for your children**

WHERE DOES ALL MY MONEY GO?

It's only two or three weeks since you've been paid and suddenly it seems your bank account is a lot lower than you thought it would be. Try as you might to account for everything you spend, it seems that, come the end of the month, you're always down to your last few pounds. There are two things you can do about this money pit, where cash disappears, never to be seen again. You could:

- £ **accept that the lifestyle you have means you are always going to have money that goes astray – maybe think about saving a bit instead**
- £ **try to do something about it instead of becoming stressed**

WHAT KIND OF MONEY PIT DO YOU HAVE?

The 'comfort zone' money pit Sometimes you just take your salary for granted, especially if you've been in the same job for several years. You feel you're doing all right moneywise, and haven't got loads of debts, so keeping tabs on your spending can take a low priority in the scheme of things.

'I'd look at my mini-statement halfway through the month and I often swear to myself that surely my bank had got it wrong,' says Louise. 'I always, always seemed to be about a hundred pounds down on what I thought I was.

'I reckoned I was pretty good with cash and didn't go too wild, so I never really looked in detail at my statements. Well, that was probably where all the problems started.

'After studiously looking through my bank statements I noticed that there were two things on my account that I'd never taken into account: my mobile-phone bill – which was regularly fifty pounds – and a fifty-pound-a-month endowment policy that I took out when I left college. I can't believe I'd forgotten about those things.

'The endowment turned out to be a nice surprise: even though it hadn't been doing too well in recent years, the high interest rates in the late 1980s and early 1990s meant I'd managed to save a bit.'

The 'nights out' money pit This kind of money pit happens when you start to earn more cash, and sometimes it seems as if there are simply not enough things around to spend it on.

'Hanging out with new mates in a new department at work meant I'd often go out and get bladdered,' admits John. 'What I didn't take account of was that every time we went out I was, more often than not, putting my credit card behind the bar and buying not one but several rounds. At the time I was trying to impress my colleagues. I didn't really notice how much cash I was spending till I got my statements.'

The 'it doesn't count: it's only cheap' money pit This is the kind of spending habit that is very difficult to keep tabs on because it tends to be the cash-only kind of spending. It's also the kind of spending that you mentally dismiss because it seems so trivial.

'I love chemist shops like Boots and Superdrug,' Imogen enthuses. 'The gimmicky girlie things – sparkly gel, hair clips and all the three-for-one offers they tend to have – makes spending money in there seem like a treat. But if you add it all up you could be spending as much as twenty pounds on fripperies a week.'

The 'lifestyle' money pit This comes with working weird hours, when spare time is spent catching up with your mates and when trawling around the supermarket seems like something you did as a child. A life of fast food, eating out and dumping clothes at the dry cleaner or getting your shirts ironed there – these are all money eaters.

A lifestyle money pit might even gobble up other more expensive things, such as a gym membership you never use, a car that goes unused, or a fine for a video you rented but never had time to take back.

'I never shop in the supermarket because even though I live in a town I'm normally too knackered when I get home,' says Jon. 'My local grocery store is open twenty-four hours but charges a third more on basics like washing powder. But, like I said, I'm too knackered to care.'

The 'clothes' money pit Fashion's a fickle thing and you should bear that in mind even when you think you're buying a bargain. If you wear it only once, even if it costs £20, it certainly is not a bargain. Fashion victims aren't called that just because of the clothes they wear: their wallets often bear the brunt of their unsuitable purchases.

How to fill your money pit, or at least stop it getting too big

- £   Become aware of how you spend your money: sometimes just being conscious of how you spend can help you save cash.
- £   Look at curbing your spending: staying in a couple of nights a week could shave off £50 if you have been a tad too generous in the pub.
- £   Think ahead: try to make time to go to the supermarket or visit your local market stall to pick up cheaper food, and ask yourself when buying clothes if you really are going to be wearing it in six months' time.
- £   Keep an eye on your bank account: if you see a regular direct debit for £20 and you don't know where it's going, check it out!

FURTHER INFORMATION

Chapters 1 and 2 have covered the basics, and looked further at debt, but you may want to know more. Here are details of some experts and how you can contact them.

The Office of Fair Trading
Fleetbank House
2–6 Salisbury Square
London EC4Y 8JX
0845 7224 499
www.oft.gov.uk.

The Consumer Credit Counselling Service (for all matters relating to credit)
freephone 0800 138 1111

National Debtline
0808 808 4000.

Citizens' Advice Bureaux
(for local numbers, see the phone book)
www.nacab.org.uk.

The Student Loans Company
100 Bothwell Street
Glasgow G2 7JD
0800 405010
www.slc.co.uk.

The National Union of Students
Nelson Mandela House
461 Holloway Road
London N7 6LJ
020 7272 8900
www.nusonline.co.uk.

National Union of Students Scotland
29 Forth Street
Edinburgh EH1 3LE
0131 556 6598
email nus-scot@dircon.co.uk.

National Union of Students-Union of Students in Ireland (NUS-USI)
29 Bedford Street
Belfast BT2 7EJ 028 9024 4641
email info@nistudents.com.

National Union of Students Wales (Undeb Cenedlaethol Myfyrwyr Cymru)
Windsor House
Windsor Lane
Cardiff CF10 3DE
029 2037 5980
email office@nus-wales.org.uk.

Association of British Credit Unions (for information on setting up or joining a credit union)
0161 832 3694.

The Insolvency Service
PO Box 203
21 Bloomsbury Street
WC1B 3QW
0121 698 4268
www.insolvency.gov.uk.

3 SAVING

WHEN SAVING REALLY WAS CHILD'S PLAY

As youngsters we were encouraged by our parents to put all our spare pennies, fivepenny pieces and even halfpennies (remember those?) into a magic money box that a few months later suddenly morphed into anything from a box of Lego, to a Sindy Doll, a Hornby locomotive or a bag of sweets and Cherry Coke.

Parents weren't the only ones in on the act: the banks and building societies were in on it, too. There was the NatWest Piggy Bank Family – mum, dad, sister, brother and baby – and the Lloyds Black Horse Young Saver's Account, where you got a free pad, pencil and horse-head-shaped moneybox.

Nowadays the art of saving is a little different. Forget the funky dictionary and personal organiser (hands up if you've still got your Midland's Griffin Account Oxford version): instead you get grown-up gimmicks such as tax breaks and high interest rates.

SAVING VERSUS INVESTING

This chapter will help you if you are looking to save your cash. If you want to invest a large one-off sum of money – say you have inherited money or won the Lotto – take a look at **How (Maybe) to Make Pots More**, too.

WHY SAVE?

£   Freedom. Having a financial cushion of some sort will give you independence and freedom. If you want to change your job or set up your own business, having cash put aside can give you the incentive to change your life.

£   Planning. Saving money can also help out when the unexpected comes along. It's like preparing for some of life's wonderful but sometimes unplannable things, such as a new baby.

£   Rainy days. Losing your job, having to take a demotion, finding yourself with a leaky and expensive roof to replace – all are rainy-day scenarios. If you've got money put aside, these things don't seem so bad.

£   Security. If you've been in the position of owing cash for most of your teens and twenties, having a few quid in the bank can be a rather comforting and warming experience. It means you can afford to go on holiday and splash out on some of life's luxuries.

£   For the sheer hell of having money. Some people do function a lot better when they know they've got more money in the bank than they know what to do with.

£   To save cash. Just because you want to save.

CAN I REALLY AFFORD TO SAVE?

With so many things to *spend* our cash on – see **Spending It** – making sure you *save* can seem like a fairly low priority. It's one of those things you think you should be doing but never seem to get down to – until now. By the way, if you have held on to your NatWest piggy bank you might like to know that a complete family set of five was sold at an auction in early 2002 for £600.

As children that £1 saved per week might not have seemed much, but watching it build up and then being able to blow it all on a trip to the toy shop made saving seem pretty cool. If you are serious about saving or you've got something specific to save up for, you need to think about putting a significant amount aside in a similar way.

WHAT ARE YOU ARE SAVING FOR?

What do you really need? Are you still fancy-free looking to go on an all-expenses cruise or a trip round the world? Are you looking to put down some roots? Or are you about to start a family?

How much should you be saving? Well, that depends on what you're saving for. Here are a few pointers.

£   For a rainy day. This is not serious saving, but it is saving nonetheless. You should probably think about putting about 5 per cent of your salary away. If you have a luxury holiday in mind for your rainy-day fund to cope with, you may want to save more. If it's a stereo or computer parts you have in mind, you could get away with saving less.

£   Deposit for a home or a wedding. This is more serious saving, depending on how long into the future you are planning for. A home is, in most cases, the single most expensive thing we purchase, while weddings don't come cheap, either. If you're planning on putting a deposit down on a home in the next year you're going to start having to think about putting aside large chunks of your salary; whereas, if it's more a five-year plan, then you're still going to need to put aside cash, just not as much.

£   My retirement. See Getting Old.

The 10 per cent rule A deposit for your first home is a very different cup of tea from a new car or wardrobe – clothes included. As a rule try to save around 10 per cent of your wages; and if you happen to come into any extra money try to put away 10 per cent of that too.

WHERE SHOULD I BE SAVING?

Spare cash aside, only you can decide how much to save. A good guide will be your age and how risky you want to be. Ask yourself how much you can afford to save and for how long. Do you want to tie your money up for years and years, or do you want to keep it somewhere where you can get instant access to it? Or do you mind putting it somewhere where you might need to give a month's notice before you need it?

But by far the most important thing you need to decide is how risky you want to be with your savings.

How risky are you? The more financial commitments you have, the less risky you can afford to be, because your money is already tied up in paying off a mortgage or a loan.

What's risky, what's not? The safest place for cash is a bog-standard instant-access deposit account, because you can get at your money straightaway and it's not tied up in any long-term plans.

The riskiest place is in anything linked to the stock market. These investments are linked to share prices, which tend to go up *and* down on a day-to-day basis.

How safe are banks and building societies? Everyone's heard the tale about the old man who kept his money under the bed. Well, for every urban myth, there's a grain of truth.

Elizabeth's father is one of those who'd rather trust a car salesman than a financial institution. 'My dad does not trust the banks or the building societies so he keeps it all in a safe at home,' she says. 'He's convinced that is really the safest place for it. It's amazing how different the attitudes of different generations are to money. I've got all my savings in stock market investments. He tells me I'm mad.'

Putting your cash in a bank account, savings or otherwise, does not guarantee you'll get it back. There is always the chance, no matter how small, that the bank you invest your money with will go belly up. There are good examples of such things happening. The Bank of Credit and Commerce International (BCCI) went under spectacularly in the early 1990s, leaving some account holders without a penny.

Most British banks are fairly safe, though, because large corporations own them and they have large backers who are prepared to stump up their own money if times get tough.

WHAT'S YOUR SAVINGS PROFILE?

Remember that this is only intended as a guide. If you don't feel comfortable putting your money somewhere – don't. First it covers the options for short-term saving, then moves on to the longer term, examining the safe, through medium-risky to the high-risk options.

Short-term saving: Safe options

Instant access savings accounts. These are handy little things that pay a small amount of interest on amounts of cash ranging from £1 to £100,000 – although the more money you want to save the longer you should think about putting it away for. You can open one with a bank, a building society, a supermarket (Sainsbury and Tesco do them with very decent interest rates) or even on the Internet. Shop around for a decent interest rate, though: you'll be able to check the current rates in the personal-finance best-buy tables published in the *Guardian* or the *Daily Telegraph* on a Saturday or Sunday. Lynda says, 'Steve, my husband, has been putting ten pounds a month into a National Savings investment account since he was a kid. It doesn't sound like a lot, but when we checked the balance it was worth £15,000. That's not bad for an amount that you don't miss.'

Regular savings accounts. These pay a slightly higher rate of interest than an instant-access account in order to encourage savers to leave their cash in for longer. You might even get a bonus interest payment if you make, say, fewer than five withdrawals a year. Like the instant-access accounts, they normally come with a bank card. You can check the rate of interest by taking a weekly look at the best-buy tables or by logging on to the Moneyfacts website (www.moneyfacts.co.uk), which gives up-to-the-minute interest rates on savings accounts.

Short-term saving: Medium- to long-term risk

Individual savings accounts (ISAs). If you are thinking about saving for only a couple of years, a cash-only ISA is a really good bet because, unlike with the other savings accounts, you don't pay tax on any interest you earn. For more information about ISAs see below.

In it for the long term If you are saving for three years or more you can afford – literally – to look at some very different types of savings.

Long-term saving: Safer options

Notice accounts. These are accounts run by banks and building societies that pay a larger amount of interest than instant-access accounts. Often you have to put in at least £100 and if you want to get it out you have to give between thirty and ninety days' notice. The interest rate you get is linked to the Bank of England's base rate – see later. This interest rate can change.

Term accounts or bonds. These savings plans often start with minimum deposit of £1,000 or more and you can't get at your money, save to close the account, for the 'term', which can be one or two years. If you can make withdrawals, you may get charged a penalty. You can choose how you get paid interest, either monthly or yearly. The interest rate on these kinds of term account tends to be fixed for the 'term'.

Guaranteed savings bonds. You'll probably have to tie up your money for a while. Remember that you are effectively acting as a lender to the bank while the money is being used to fund their investment or expansion plans. The word 'guaranteed' means that you will get back the original money you invested – so long as the bank you are investing the money with doesn't go bust.

Long-term saving: Medium-risk options

Stock-market-linked bonds. The longer you put your cash away for and the riskier you want to be, the more serious a saver you are. Most stock market savings plans require £1,000 or more to start and, as with the term account above, you normally can't get at your money until the end of the term, which can be between one and five years.

These accounts pay interest according to how well a particular stock market does. This is done by calculating the average increase in the value of all the companies listed on the stock market to which you have chosen to link your casings (you can choose Tokyo or anywhere else if you wish, but the most common choice is London for UK savers). The interest you get is usually less than the full increase in the index. If the index falls during the time you invest, you just get back the amount you invested and no interest at all. These kinds of account let you dabble in the stock market without losing the cash you put in at the beginning.

The question you have to ask, of course, is whether the stock market is the place for you. If you don't mind gambling with your cash, the longer you invest it for, the more suitable a candidate you are for a more risky stocks-and-shares-based investment. It's not the same as buying individual shares, though: you are not buying into individual companies and you are spreading your bets on the performance of a whole country or industry within that country. Stock-market-linked bonds are a good starter account if you are interested in shares.

Long-term saving: High-risk options

Corporate bonds. These are stock market investments but they tend to invest in one company and you may not get all your cash back at the end. They are not like shares and tend to be avoided by ordinary savers.

INDIVIDUAL SAVINGS ACCOUNTS

If you want to invest your money in the stock market you may be best off with an ISA – a tax-free savings and shares account that was set up by Chancellor Gordon Brown in 1999. These accounts are great whether you are saving a small or large amount of cash and whether you want to take a risk or not take a risk with your cash.

If you don't want to have your money cooped up for five years, but you're still interested in gambling with it, then an instant-access ISA is a good bet.

Background on ISAs ISAs replaced personal equity plans (PEPs) and tax-exempt special savings accounts (TESSAs) as tax-free savings plans for the masses. They were introduced to encourage the public to invest in the stock market without having to worry about paying tax.

An ISA is often described as being the tax-free wrapper: all you have to do is choose what you want to go inside it. You can choose to buy shares, put in cash or use your life-insurance contributions. You can even choose a mix of all three.

What can I put into an ISA? There are three components of ISAs.

- £   A stocks-and-shares ISA allows you to invest as little as £50 or as much as £7,000 – good for long- to medium-term savings.
- £   If you just want a cash ISA, you can put in between £1,000 and £3,000 a year – this is good for short- or long-term savings.
- £   You can put up to £1,000 a year into a life-insurance ISA. Remember that, because they do have an investment element, life-insurance policies are more risky than cash, and because it is an insurance policy you may not see the money you do put away (see A Little Bit of Protection for details on life insurance).

All these limits have been set until 5 April 2006.

More rules on ISAs The maximum amount you can put into any ISA (or any combination of ISAs) is £7,000 a year. So, if you decide to put £7,000 into a stocks-and-shares ISA, you won't be able to open up a cash or a life-insurance ISA. If you decide to put £3,000 into a cash ISA you will have only £4,000 left to put into a shares ISA, or £3,000 if you put a further £1,000 into a life-insurance ISA.

Mini and maxi ISAs A lot of financial companies talk about mini and maxi ISAs. That's because they offer ISAs that allow a mix of shares, cash and life insurance.

'Maxi' refers to the maximum amount you can put in your ISA, so a maxi ISA is one that allows you to put the whole £7,000 limit into it. To be called 'maxi' it must therefore allow you to put in shares as well as cash.

A mini ISA is the name given to the separate types of ISA. You can have three mini ISAs, one with cash, one with shares and one with life insurance.

Anton has taken out his ISA for the long term after he was financially burned. He explains why. 'The first year they came out I put in my whole allowance. I had got a one-off bonus from an IT project and wanted to save as much of it as possible. I put three thousand pounds into the cash bit and it did really, really well, but the rest I put into a share fund that invested in IT stocks. This did well in 1999 but did not do so well in 2001 and 2002. All I can do is hope that the market gets better because at the moment my four-thousand-pound bit is only worth about three thousand pounds.'

Share ISAs Multi-share or unit-trust ISAs have themes that allow you to choose which stocks and shares you buy. You can put your money into an ISA that invests in the shares of the top 100 UK companies (these are known as the FTSE 100) or, if you wish, you can put your cash into an ISA with an Asian or South American theme.

Special shares: pick and mix You don't have to put all your permitted £7,000 into the same shares ISA, so, if you fancy putting your cash into something that invests in South American stocks as well as UK ones, you've got a choice. Because lots of people want to spread their share-ISA money, financial companies have set up fund 'supermarkets', where you can go and choose which stocks and shares you want to mix and match. A lot of these fund supermarkets are on the Internet, so you can check out what's around to buy before you commit your cash.

What about existing PEPs and TESSAs? ISAs replaced PEPs and TESSAs on 6 April 1999. If you have a PEP or TESSA bought before that date you can continue to hold the account, but you cannot put in any new money and any interest you do start earning may be liable to tax again.

If you have a PEP Although you have not been able to put in any new money into your PEP since April 1999, any returns can be reinvested in the PEP or withdrawn. You can also transfer part or all of any PEP to another PEP manager.

If you have a TESSA You can continue to put money into your TESSA until your account matures. When it does mature, you have six months to transfer the capital (just what you put in and not the interest, which you have to take as cash) to a special 'TESSA-only' ISA. If you don't, you may have to start paying tax on the interest in your original TESSA. The money you put in does not count towards your ISA allowance, either. If you wish, you can put your TESSA money into a cash-only allowance – and remember that you don't have to keep your money in the same bank or building society: you can shop around for another TESSA-only ISA using the rates in Moneyfacts.

What's really so special about an ISA When the government introduced ISAs it also introduced standards or CAT marks (CAT stands for 'charges, access and terms'). Not all ISAs have CAT standards, but those that do have to offer savers special terms.

A cash ISA with a CAT mark will have to have

£   **no extra charges – your money is not being actively managed so you should not be paying anything other than your savings into the account**
£   **small savings – you can put in or take out as little as £10 with less than a week's notice**
£   **good interest – one that is never more than 2 per cent lower than the Bank of England's base rates**

Life-insurance ISAs with CAT marks have to have

£   **low annual charges – they must be no more than 3 per cent of the fund value**
£   **small savings – you should be able to pay in as little as £25 a month or £250 a year**
£   **no penalty – you should receive at least all the premiums that you paid for three years or more before the date you cash it in**

Stocks-and-shares ISAs with CAT marks should have

£   **low charges – annual management charge must be no more than 1 per cent of your fund value**
£   **no other charges – some investment plans involving shares may have**

other charges, such as for taking your money out at short notice (see
How (Maybe) to Make Pots More)

£   small savings – as little as £50 a month, or a minimum lump sum of £500

Do you have to put in £7,000 in one go? A we have seen, lots of
share ISAs will let you put in from £1 a month. But remember that
some of your share-ISA cash will get gobbled up in charges: unit-
trust and OEIC ISAs (these are open-ended investment company
accounts and are explained in **How (Maybe) to Make Pots More)**
need to pay fund managers to organise the investment – so it may
make sense to put more in.

What does the tax-free thing mean? If you have a cash ISA you will
get all your interest tax-free, so you make more interest than you
would in a normal savings account. If you have a share ISA, the tax-
free bit means that any dividends (the income that shares make), or
any other money the shares make, is all paid to you gross. With a
life-insurance ISA you don't pay tax on the bonuses you get.

Who offers ISAs? Almost any financial company offers ISAs. As
well as banks, building societies and supermarkets, you can buy an
ISA direct from an investment house (the people who manage the
shares) and even off the Internet.

Should I go to a financial adviser? ISAs can be as simple or as
complicated as you want to make them. But, as with all savings,
the more risky you want to be the more research you may have to
do, and that may mean you have to buy your ISA – if it's a share one
– through an adviser. Remember that advisers do charge for their
services. They do this by either taking commission out of the
management charge you pay the ISA company, or through a fee.
The fee will be something that you pay the adviser direct, and they
will normally tell you how much this is when you first visit them.
You need to shop around for an adviser who will suit you.

GETTING INTO THE SAVINGS HABIT

There are many savings accounts around, but it's one thing to open
one and quite another to start putting your cash away, especially if
you are all too tempted to live in the here and now.

If you really, really can't be trusted with your savings, and you can't afford to tie it up for years on end, there are loads of other options – including postal accounts. These often come without cash cards, so the temptation to dip into your savings is removed. They will also come with a strict limit on how much notice you have to give if you want the money out.

WHAT ABOUT OTHER SAVINGS ACCOUNTS?

If that hasn't inspired you to save, then you may be better off looking at investing your money. Investing means taking more of a risk with your money, and will mean you have to start doing a bit of homework. Savings shouldn't ...

£ **Leave you out of pocket. If you're paying off heavy debts, then you're probably better off waiting until you've cleared them before you start saving. There's no point putting £100 cash into an account paying 10 per cent interest when your credit card is charging you 18 per cent.**

£ **Cost you too much. Savings don't always come free. If you've gone for a stock-market-linked investment, such as an ISA, then you simply have to read the small print. These investments will levy a small charge for managing your money – that's because they are a more 'active' savings account than an ordinary post office account.**

£ **Bamboozle you. You need to make sure you get regular statements letting you know how your cash is doing, and the company managing your savings should always let you know when the interest rate changes.**

£ **Insist on taking more than they should. You can save just £1 a month if you wish. Never feel pressurised into opening a savings account that insists you put in a minimum of £100. If you can't afford it, and you're not comfortable doing it – this is worth repeating – don't. It's your hard-earned cash and you can do with it what you like.**

GET THE MOST OUT OF YOUR SAVINGS

Don't just invest and then forget about your savings account. Interest rates change all the time. Check frequently that you are still getting a good return on your money. If you're not, switch to a new account – but watch out for any penalties or loss of interest on closing the old account. This does not apply to term accounts, from which you can't usually withdraw your money before the end of the set term.

The personal-finance pages of newspapers, personal-finance magazines and consumer magazines such as *Which?* often print details of best-buy savings accounts. From time to time they also publish reports comparing current accounts. If you have access to the Internet, check out an information-laden site like Moneyfacts (www.moneyfacts.co.uk), which will allow you to check at a glance what accounts are paying the best, and worst, rates of interest.

But beware: best-buy tables for the stock-market ISAs will give you a past-performance indication, but that doesn't mean it will do so well in the future. With stocks-and-shares ISAs you'll need to gen up on the kinds of investments you're thinking of buying.

SPREAD YOUR BETS

Don't put all your money into one basket. If you've got a high-interest, fairly risky savings account, try to balance it with another less risky one.

Anton, see above, adds, 'After getting my fingers burned, and my wallet, with my IT shares I decided to take out a post office investment account. I don't put a lot into it but I do feel that at least some of my cash is safe.'

WHAT ELSE CAN I DO TO SAVE MONEY?

Even if you are putting only a small amount into a savings account you're still saving. And don't dismiss the old piggy-bank idea entirely: popping a pound into an old bottle is not such a bad habit to get into.

The small details certainly mattered to Maria when she left a city job to become a teacher. 'When I had been well paid I'd stashed the odd pound coin, as well as the five- and tenpenny pieces, in my savings jar,' she says. 'Of course, I'd been well paid before, so that kind of money had not mattered, but it soon came in handy when I was scrabbling around for dinner and Tube fares.'

WHEN YOU'RE TEMPTED TO DIP INTO YOUR SAVINGS

Spending is an addictive habit, so there may be times when you have to do 'cold turkey' and remind yourself of why you are saving up in the first place.

£   You want to be able to treat yourself and your family without worrying about next month's credit-card bill.
£   It can give you choices – you don't always have to opt for the cheapest thing if you've got a bit of spare cash.
£   If you can save money, think of all the other things you can do with it – you might even get enough together to think about investing.
£   Having a deposit for a home can shave hundreds of pounds off a mortgage.
£   You can't always live now and pay later.

HOW THE OTHER HALF SAVE

Being frugal with your cash is another way of saving. The Virgin boss Richard Branson put all his pocket money into setting up a magazine, as did *Dennis* magazine's flamboyant founder Felix Dennis – both are now worth millions.

OTHER KINDS OF SAVINGS

It's not just cash that can make you money. There are other things that could be right under your nose, and worth a fortune. Here are some bits and pieces but there are probably a lot more.

ART

That kitsch picture hanging in the kitchen could be worth millions – well, thousands, maybe. Look at the pictures of 'the Orphans' – the sad youngsters whose mournful faces adorned the picture frames of cafés and greasy-spoon establishments everywhere in the late seventies and early eighties. These were worth cash because someone, somewhere, was collecting them. Some of the kitsch Athena posters that graced school folders are now considered modern art.

Buying art as an investment is something many celebrities do – Madonna and Mick Jagger have been known to spend hundreds of thousands on paintings and sculptures that are worth even more.

ANTIQUES

If it's over 25 years old, in short supply and in demand, it's probably an antique. Look at the NatWest piggies, for example. If you need some inspiration check *The Antiques Roadshow*: that old rubbish you have been pleading with your dad to get rid of could be worth something.

CLOTHES

If you really need a bit more cash, then selling your old clothes to a dress agency may give you a bit of extra money (see also **Spending It**). 'I had an Ozzy Clark dress which was over twenty-five years old,' says Jacqui. 'I sold it to a dress agency for a hundred pounds because the designer had died and his stuff was considered to be almost antique. When I bought it, it was only twenty-five pounds – although that seemed a huge amount at the time.'

EVERYDAY BILLS

Have you thought of switching your phone, gas and electricity companies? British Gas is no longer the main, or necessarily the cheapest, supplier of gas in the UK. Since the government deregulated electricity and gas supply, many new companies have begun to offer cheaper services. Some companies will combine your phone, gas, electricity and even cable TV services, so you pay just the one bill. This can work out a lot cheaper, but do get a quote first. Obtain details of local suppliers at your local library. Remember that gas and electricity companies are answerable to regulators, so they cannot stop you from switching.

You can go online to have a look at how much you can save, too. A company called MoneySupermarket offers online comparisons. It offers an online calculator to compare prices at www.moneysupermarket.com, or you can look up how green the energy you are using is on http://compare-prices-online.co.uk/utility-companies/ or www.uSwitch.com.

If you are visited by salespeople from rival gas and electricity companies, check what you are signing. Helen, a student, has this cautionary story. 'A woman came round our street offering us cheaper gas and electricity,' she says. 'She said I needed to sign a form to get the quote and assured me that that was all I was doing, and she was very pushy. Next thing I know we'd actually had our electricity and gas switched over. Apparently, the agreement I'd signed was for switching, not just a quote.

'Well, I was so annoyed with the company that I opted to switch it back. It took ages, though, and at the end of the day the electricity and gas weren't any cheaper.'

Pushy salespeople aside, switching your gas and electricity can still be a good move, and it may not be just money that you save. Pheobe, an IT saleswoman, says, 'We were given the offer of switching our supplier to a green tariff. This meant that the gas and electricity came from a renewable source. We compared our bill and we had saved forty pounds in a year.'

SWITCHING YOUR CURRENT ACCOUNT

If you haven't done so already, check **Spending It** for details on how switching your bank account might not just save, but may also make, you money.

Doing your homework If you are going to turn into a savings bunny you will be needing some of these numbers.

Moneyfacts is the best place to start if you want to keep an eye on the most favourable rates of interest. It is best to look at the website, www.moneyfacts.co.uk, but if you do not have access to the Internet you can order the *Moneyfacts* publication by calling the subscription hotline on 01603 476476.

The **Research Department** provides many statistics that are used in the national papers and financial magazines. Its website address is www.trd.co.uk.

The **Inland Revenue**'s ISA helpline on 0845 604 1701 is open between 8.30 a.m. and 5 p.m., Monday to Thursday, and between 8.30 a.m. and 4.30 p.m. on Fridays.

If you feel you may have been cheated out of your rightful savings, or have been charged too much for financial services, try the **Financial Ombudsman Service**, which helps to resolve complaints between savers and financial firms (0845 080 1800; www.financial-ombudsman.org.uk).

Happy saving.

4 MONEY AND RELATIONSHIPS

WHEN MONEY IS NO LONGER CHILD'S PLAY

Money, whether too much, not enough or even just enough, complicates relationships. That's because a lot of us learn from a very young age how good an emotional bargaining tool money can be. Remember being persuaded to forsake a game of lightsabers to clean the car when your parents offered you a few pence extra pocket money?

Money is used by older brothers and sisters to bribe younger siblings either to keep quiet or to take a hike. Parents use pocket money to persuade reluctant ten-year-olds to do the washing up, while aunts, uncles and grandparents often use money to help make up for lost time, or in lieu of a present for a missed birthday.

As children get older they soon learn to up the ante, using homework, end-of-term reports or sports day to extract money from parents or family. It no longer becomes a straight exchange, but the promise of something – hard work – that marks their cash relationship with their parents.

Along the way they sometimes forget the emotional impact of their financial wants. Accepting money that is the by-product of a bargain is a tacit agreement with the emotional terms of the giver. This becomes even more apparent as intimate relationships become as much about bill-sharing as sex or romantic nights out.

Ignore the money issue at your peril: money is the major cause of relationship break-ups. Money is a major sticking patch because no two people share exactly the same attitude to cash – in fact most of us are fairly ambiguous, shifting between stinginess ('It's too expensive') and outright generosity ('I saw it and thought of you').

FRIENDS AND MONEY

How do you cope when friendship and money do not seem to go well together? Have a look at a few common friendship/money dilemmas. Recognise any?

TO GO POSH – OR NOT TO GO POSH

You want to go to a cheap restaurant but your mate has got his or her bonus and wants to go somewhere where a bottle of house red adds up to a day's wages – namely yours.

If you want to stay friends you're going to have to accept going for broke at times. If it's a special occasion like a birthday then a takeaway from the local pizza house will miss the culinary spot. If it's just an after-work nosh then you're going to have to steer your mate away from the à la carte menu. Remember that lots of posh eateries do have set meals that allow you to eat for a fraction of the normal price.

YOU EARN MORE THAN THEY DO

You've been working hard for years, watching your mates earn good money, and then suddenly – hey presto! – you are the one with bottomless pockets. Should you end up paying for them every time you go out? Should you be buying them gifts to make up for your good luck?

No, not unless you've won the Lotto, when it is your statutory right to spread a little of your good luck around. It doesn't take a career consultant to know that you've probably been working damned hard to get that extra money, and your friends – if they are friends – will know this, too. There may be occasions when you do feel like simply treating your mates because they've been so supportive. This is OK, too. And remember: you shouldn't push them to do more expensive things than they are happy doing.

Anthony, who is now a graphic designer, found himself in this situation. 'I used to be the poor one among the group,' he says. 'When we lived in flats at university it was me who was always scrounging around for food and beer – even more galling because one of my flatmates used to cook steak nearly every night. Then, about two years after we left university, two years during which I was always the one who was broke when we went out, I finally landed the job I wanted – decent salary, too.

'My new salary changed a few dynamics. We had always gone to cheap restaurants to stop making me feel broke, but now we could afford to go to pricier places. The first few times we went out I bought lots of drinks but it got to be a bit of a joke the way I was flashing my cash around. I soon realised that, though I was earning more than my mates, I still had to look after the pennies.'

But what if you have always had lots of money?

'I was the one in Anthony's flat who had steak every night,' admits Sara. 'I bought lots of rounds of drinks, too, because I was in the lucky situation of having rich parents. But once I left university I had to be extra careful. Friends start expecting things and I notice that there are people who don't hang out with me now because they don't get a free ride.'

To flaunt it or not If you do suddenly earn more, bear in mind that not everyone else, even your closest mate, is going to want to be constantly reminded of your good fortune. What do you do?

Iain felt his mate could have done with a few lessons on financial tact. 'I'd been made redundant,' he says. 'My best mate had got a promotion, with a five-grand rise to boot. He acted liked lord and master for about five weeks, constantly talking about the new car he was going to get – guess what: he got a new car as part of the package. He started going to city bars where beer was three pounds a bottle – I mean, I'll only pay that in clubs. It all came to a head when he suggested we go out with his mates, who earn loads as well. We had a great big row and didn't speak to each other for months.'

THEY EARN MORE THAN YOU DO

This is when the green-eyed destroyers of friendships, jealousy and envy, rear their nasty heads. Feeling eaten up over a friend's promotion will do you no favours.

There are two things you can do when this happens: avoid your mate until you've got over it; or use your friend's success as an inspiration.

It's not just about earning, though: sometimes our mates come into money, but not through hard work of their own.

'Pat got given ten thousand pounds by her parents to help her out when she was in the second year of university,' says Amanda. 'There I was completely struggling and already with six thousand pounds of loans and credit cards. It was really tough dealing with it because it was so hard for me. Luckily, she's a good mate and the first thing she did with the cash was take me out for a meal. It showed she cared and that friendships are more important than money.'

SHOULD YOU LEND YOUR MATES MONEY?

Shakespeare's advice in *Hamlet*, 'Neither a borrower nor a lender be', hasn't stood the test of time for nothing. It depends on how much you want to lend to your mate. A tenner is OK but if you've got friends asking for multiples of £50 or more you're going to have to go easy. If your friend is asking for this kind of cash on a regular basis, chances are they owe money to someone else, such as the bank or a credit card. You don't have to confront them, but it may be a good idea, over a drink or a coffee, to ask them if they are having any cash-flow difficulties.

FLATMATES AND HOUSEMATES

The loose, often blurry relationship you have with friends over money becomes a more formalised one once you start sharing bills and rent. If someone isn't pulling their financial weight in a household it makes life very difficult for the cohabitants.

Should you share with friends? The jury is out on this one because it's not just the loo-seat issue but the much bigger money issue that can make sharing with mates hell, or heaven.

Kerri is opting to live on her own. 'I would never, ever share with a friend again,' she avows. 'Every time I've lived in a flat with a mate it hasn't worked out. Because your relationship is intense to start with you can often find yourself arguing about really stupid things, or you end up bitching about your other mates. Chances are you are familiar with your mate's bad habits so they'll only end up annoying you even more when you live with them.'

Cara, a postgraduate student, disagrees. 'I think sharing with my mates was one of the best things I did,' she says. 'After we left college we all got jobs in Manchester and, as friendly as the city is compared to London, it can still feel a bit lonely. Four of us shared a house and it was the best year I've ever had. We did have a couple of squabbles and they were over unpaid bills. But it all got sorted in the end.'

SPLITTING THE BILLS

This is when everything should get split between all the housemates. If one of you is not in the house as much as the others, maybe staying with a boyfriend or girlfriend, then they should still have to pay their share of the bills and council tax.

GUIDE TO A HAPPY HOUSE SHARE

Have a kitty Set up a separate bank account for household expenses and all arrange for cash to go into the account. You all pay the same amount when you get paid, or get your loan if you're a student. Arrange to sit down together once a month to organise your bills. The meeting will also give you time to discuss any other important issues.

Pay bills by direct debit It's certainly cheaper. The TV-licensing people, electricity companies and gas companies offer reductions for customers who pay via direct debit. But one person will have to take responsibility for the payment of that bill, which can be a bit difficult when it comes to chasing up your other housemates. It's worth doing, but only with housemates you've known for a while. Council-tax payments are easier to handle: your local council will let you all pay independently via a standing order so that one person doesn't have to take sole responsibility.

Make sure all utility companies know that the household is a shared one, and get all your names to appear on the bills. That's because it's the responsibility of the person whose name is on the bill to pay.

SHARING THE RENT

If it's between all housemates and the landlord (see **Building a Nest** for details on renting), then it's up to all of you to make sure the rent is paid, unless it states otherwise in your rental agreement. It's time to read the small print again!

Andrea and her flatmate Samuel didn't. 'We rented a house near Bicester for a thousand pounds a month,' she says. 'There were four of us, so it worked out at around two hundred and fifty pounds each. Within six months two of the blokes had been made redundant and had to move out back home. We couldn't get people in to fill the rooms immediately. The landlord was still insisting on the full whack, so me and my housemate had to cough up between us. That was harsh. We had to do that for two months, but we did not want to lose the house.'

RENTING RULES

£   Paperwork is tedious but, by keeping a record of your rental payments, you'll be protecting yourself against a dispute with your landlord.
£   Communication with your landlord is important, so, if you are having trouble, let your landlord know. They may be more understanding than you think.
£   Cash is good, so have an emergency cash fund to pay for the unexpected and it'll also give you something when you want to pay for parties.
£   Pay your way, because getting behind with the bills will lead to resentment.

PUTTING BREAD ON THE TABLE

Having a kitty for basics such as milk, tea and coffee is good in theory, but doesn't always work. 'We tried the kitty idea,' says one house sharer, Simon, 'but we had one guy in the house who was always, always broke and would think nothing of dipping into the house fund box. He ended up leaving and the guy who came in next earned more and was more generous. You have to be prepared to pay your share and stick to it.'

IF SOMEONE DOES A RUNNER

Everyone knows someone with a housemate-from-hell story, and it normally involves money. Rebecca still remembers one such housemate. 'Melvyn left the house owing me around fifty pounds because I'd paid up front for his share of the bills,' she says. 'When he left I never bothered chasing him for that share. I still remember it now and if I see him I'll still ask him for it. That was five years ago!'

GETTING YOUR MONEY BACK

There is a legal way you can get your money back, whether it's an unpaid deposit from a dodgy landlord or a former housemate – the small-claims court. You need proof of the amount owed and the address of the person who owes the money. A solicitor, or better still your local Citizens' Advice Bureau, will help you. Lodging a small claim will cost you around £50 but you'll get that back if your claim is successful.

MONEY AND YOUR FAMILY

STILL LIVING AT HOME?

It's getting very expensive to buy your own home. Thousands of twentysomethings, and even early-thirtysomethings, are heading back to their families to try to save cash. It makes financial sense: paying a landlord hundreds of pounds when you're trying to save up the money for your own pad can end up draining vital finances, especially when the average house costs over £100,000.

RULES FOR LIVING AT HOME

Doing time Try to set a time limit on your stay: it will probably make your family feel better and will reassure them that you are intending to fly the nest at some point.

Pay your way If your family are still working themselves, or there's still a mortgage being paid off, then your contribution to family finances will be most welcome. Sit down with your folks and work out how much the average bills are, including food, electricity, council tax and so on, and then offer to pay your share.

Give each other space Living back in the family nest can be emotionally overwhelming at times, for all of you. Agree to have 'nights off', when you won't be around.

Don't take them for granted Your parents may at times feel a bit used. It may be hard to accept but, even with the best of intentions, you are effectively using them to save yourself money. The odd thank-you card, box of chocolates or a Friday-night takeaway can work wonders to smooth a ruffled parental feather.

Being grown up Going back to live with family can actually help you grow up. If your folks see you acting responsibly with cash and learning to pay your way, then it can bring a whole new meaning to family harmony.

LOVE AND MONEY

If things in the love department are becoming serious, there's no way you can afford to ignore the cash issue. But where exactly are you in your relationship when it comes to the pound signs?

THE HONEYMOON PERIOD

Cash – like emotions – is in free-flow mode. This period can last anything from just a few weeks to a few years. This is the time when no present is too expensive, no dinner bill is too extravagant and no debt is too much to run up to please the object or your lust or love.

One man who's done a lot of spending is Si: 'I spent a fortune, well, eight hundred pounds, during the first six months with my girlfriend – now my fiancée. That was on meals, weekends away and little gifts. I'm still generous but I guess I feel that now we've become more settled I don't need to impress her so much. She's spent things on me, too, but I haven't dared ask how much her credit-card bill is – that's just not romance, is it?'

THEN BAGGAGE COMES ON BOARD, TOO

Then there's the settling-in period, when you both start testing each other to see how far one can push the other. This can be anything from six months to years. This is often the first time you row. It's also the time when you start to hold back on your spending and it can be when you start to find out just how much financial and emotional baggage your partner has amassed.

Mia, a physiotherapist, has a warning about baggage: 'My boyfriend had always been very generous with me, except, funnily enough, on our first date, when he had to ask me for the money for a cab. We moved in together after a couple of months and when I was cleaning out our cupboards I found a letter – in fact, several – from one of his exes. He had borrowed thousands off her – or, more to the point, her parents. I didn't tell him I'd seen it, but from then on I watched his attitude to cash like a hawk.

'Nearly two years into the relationship I ended up paying for a holiday. He eventually gave me the cash but it took forever. The day we broke up I even lent him a hundred and fifty pounds, which I later found out was to take his new girlfriend on a weekend break. I'm never going to be such a sucker with money and men again. I mean, all the warning signs were there.'

THE COMFY-OLD-SHOES STAGE

Then there's the comfortable bit, when you've dealt with all the serious matters such as rent and mortgage (see **Building a Nest** for more about buying with a partner), and it becomes everyday money matters such as food and bills that you deal with.

'We have managed to get a balance even though I am better with cash than her,' claims Si. 'Living together and sorting out bills can get hairy, but you simply have to deal with it, otherwise there's no heating or no shower.'

The second stage is the most dangerous financially. The cold, hard reality of paying bills and rent and buying food and clothes can cloud the romantic mist surrounding the most loving couples.

MONEY AND DATING

When you're first seeing someone money doesn't seem to matter. It may not become apparent that you're going out with a stingy type until you have to cough up for something you wouldn't expect.

But money is just as important as romance. If you care and respect someone, sorting out your finances together can be just as romantic as a weekend in Paris. It means you see yourself as having a future with that person. A future together means sorting out your money together.

DATING DILEMMAS

Should we always split the bill? This is probably an issue only at the beginning of a relationship, when you're still trying to work out whether you want to see this person or not. Lots of people suffer from a financial form of tokenism when they start dating. They figure that, since men and women are paid equally and both work, why should men feel obliged to pay for every romantic meal ever cooked?

Offering to pay Don't say anything you don't mean. If you are the one who has offered to pay, then do so. If you can't afford to foot the bill, then admit it. You don't have to tell your date you're completely broke: just make it clear from the start that you are going Dutch.

If you are the one being treated If you're the one in the lucky position of being paid for, offer only if you can afford it. Accept that your date – male or female – may want to pay for you. If you feel guilty about someone else paying the bill, then make sure you return the favour – if you want to see them again of course.

Here are a few more questions and concerns you might like to consider.

He/she wants to do expensive and I can't afford it If you are going to have a relationship together, talking about this is very important. Your potential partner will not really want to know the ins and outs of your bank account (unless they are your bank manager), just that they fancy you and that you're a great person to be with. You don't have to go all mournful on them: just explain that you'd rather go to the local Italian than the latest trendy five-star eatery. If you can find alternative suggestions that don't cost so much, then you'll be taking proactive steps to put the relationship on an equal financial footing.

You don't have to splash out on presents, either, says Iain. 'Caroline and I started going out when she was still a student and I was in my first job, so it made sense that I paid for a lot of things. Caz got a bit fed up with it, though. So on our first Christmas together she suggested that we both buy each other really simple, inexpensive presents. But we had to be really imaginative. It was great because we only spent five pounds on each other, but the things we bought were so funny: mine was a dolphin-shaped plug holder and hers was a pair of insoles for my smelly feet!'

If I owe loads of money, how far into a relationship do I tell my partner? Not until you feel comfortable, if you don't want to you don't have to.

Should I tell them how much I earn? If you earn stacks (see 'To flaunt it or not' above) and you want to tell your new hunk/hunkette, then do so – just don't expect them to be impressed. Sometimes, sharing salary details is best saved until you've been together for a while.

My date is asking me for money to get a taxi home, otherwise they want to stay at mine This is when your date's attitude to money speaks louder than a loudhailer on Brighton beach at six in the morning. Chances are they do have enough money for the taxi: don't they carry a cash card (in which case you probably should be a bit worried if they don't)? They are chancing their luck and seeing how far they can take a fledgling relationship. If you really don't want them to come back, offer to sub them the cash and then ask them why they don't have a cash card!

My new boyfriend/girlfriend doesn't have much money – should I be subbing them already? If you've found yourself in this situation before, it may be you that's stuck in a money relationship rut. If you can see a decent future in the relationship you'll need to ask yourself and your beloved several questions. Why don't they have enough money? Are they working? Have they got a previous relationship that swallows up their cash? Have they always ended up relying on past partners for money? If this is a habit of theirs, then you need to ask yourself whether you want to stay with this person. So, yes, sub them on occasions, but don't let it become a regular habit.

WHEN YOU GET SERIOUS

Your joint finances – lack of or excess of – take on a whole new meaning when you move in with each other. Most couples use living together in rented accommodation as a rehearsal for either buying together or getting married. It's a good time to check out how financially well suited you are.

Renting together If you are renting together, the rental agreement with your landlord will normally require you to commit for a minimum of six months. Before you move in, consider these points.

Discuss everything As with all relationship issues the key to happiness is communication. Don't just assume you'll be sharing bills, and don't take anything financial for granted.

Marc left money out of the conversation to his misfortune. 'She was a shopaholic. Coming home with this, that and the other,' he says. 'I told her that if we moved in together she was going to have to make sure that she put some money around for bills. Obviously her Miu Miu skirts and shoes meant a lot more to her than I ever did – we split up the next week.'

Set up a system One option is that each takes responsibility for making sure particular bills are paid. You may, for instance, offer to make sure the electricity is sorted and your partner may offer to pay the council tax.

Set up a bank account Keep a joint account for household bills and rent or mortgage, and keep your own bank account for your salary, then pay an agreed amount into the joint account each month. Make it a direct-debit, cash-only account so neither of you is tempted to go into it when things get tough.

Krispin, a web designer, points out the perils of not sorting out your cash issues. 'We bought a house together and were sharing the mortgage,' he says. 'One day I went to the cash machine to find we were massively overdrawn. She'd gone out and spent our money, on some clothes of all things. We nearly missed paying the mortgage that month.'

Have joint goals Make sure you both save together for holidays and home buying, and make sure that you save the same amount so that one of you does not have the monopoly on how the money is spent.

Be your own financial person 'Always keep your own bank account and your own income,' advises newly married Katie. 'Sharing bills is great and can really equalise a relationship that's going somewhere. I draw the line at sharing cash cards and PIN numbers. Even married couples have to have a bit of financial breathing space.'

Talk about it If you are having money troubles discuss them with your partner. You never know, they might have mistaken your fears for something else, as Danni found out.

'I owed at least six thousand pounds of student debt when I first met Simon. I didn't tell him that but it really used to get me down to the point where I had to go to the doctor for antidepressants. He wanted to do things together, like going on holiday and, more importantly, move in together.

'Because I wanted to sort myself out financially, first I kept him at arm's length. Then the crunch came – we had one of "those conversations", when he asked me how committed I was. He said that it looked like I didn't want us to move in together. We very nearly split up; in fact we agreed to separate for a week. During that time I was so miserable without him I knew I had to come clean about the money I owed.

'Once he knew, Simon even suggested I move in with him to save rent. We're now engaged and I've nearly paid off all my debts.'

But don't sub them – well, not all the time If your partner is downright rubbish with money, helping them out all the time is only going to make you resentful. And when you have that inevitable row chances are all the support you've given will be thrown back in your loved one's face.

'I was in a relationship where my boyfriend paid for everything,' says Vicki. 'He even gave me dinner money when I ran out of cash. At the time I was really struggling to pay off some debts, so I used to use a lot of my salary to sort myself out. I knew he'd always bail me out. So when I got paid each month I made sure all my debts were paid and then with the rest of the money I'd go and blow it all on clothes.

'I had a bit of a free ride, really, because I lived rent-free with him. When we split up I'd paid most of my debts off, but I had a real problem adjusting to having to pay my own bills again – even though it wasn't like I'd never paid them before or anything. I ended up getting into more debt and it was only because I got made redundant that I finally got free of owing cash and had some savings behind me.

'I still look back at those times and I think what a scrounger I was; but if the relationship had been going anywhere I guess he would also have wanted to address the issue.'

Some partners get a kick out of being the financial provider of the relationship. You don't want to be in a relationship where money is used as a tool to subordinate you.

Buying together The focus on most committed relationships is on living arrangements – but going from living together to buying a place is a big step. Having a mortgage means that both your finances are as irrevocably tied as you both are.

Moneywise, having a mortgage is no different from paying rent, except that this time you're both putting cash towards your own place and you have to take joint responsibility if you cannot afford to pay your monthly mortgage.

Before you move in ...

- £   You have to decide whether you're going to take a fifty-fifty share – i.e. half each – in the property.
- £   You'll also have to work out how much of a deposit you both want to put down – the larger the deposit, the more you reduce the amount you need to borrow.
- £   If you are not married you'll have to draw up some kind of a 'prenuptial' agreement that states who owns what – it may even come down to furniture.

If the other person owns and you don't If you move in to your partner's home you should still be offering to pay your share of the bills (see above). However, the rent dynamic changes because your partner is paying a mortgage. If they want you to pay towards that mortgage, you'll need to be religious in keeping records of that rental payment.

RULES TO KEEP YOURSELF FINANCIALLY AFLOAT WHEN YOU ARE IN A RELATIONSHIP

If you're renting together ...

£   Make sure you both pay your way – this will save the issue of unpaid bills/council tax.

£   Have both your names on any bills – it means not just one of you is liable.

£   Do set up a joint account – it proves you've both been paying the rent and other bills.

If only one of you has a mortgage All the rules above apply – but it's also important that you keep records of any rent you may pay your partner or any rent they pay you. If a partner is not named as being an owner of the home you live in, but can prove to have made substantial contributions (perhaps having been living there a while and paid chunks of rent and bills), then they may be entitled to a share of your home if you split up.

If you have a mortgage together Get it all down in writing. You don't have to be married to draw up a prenuptial-type agreement. Solicitors will happily help you draw up what is often called a *living-together agreement*, or a *declaration of trust*. This sets out in writing who gets what should you split up or should one of you die. This is particularly important if you or your partner has children from a previous relationship. And, while it may not stop things getting nasty if you do have a less-than-amicable split, it will give both of you a reference point to bargain with.

WILLS

Things can get very complicated when one of you dies. Making sure that you have a will can be a way of getting round the nasty agreement business. It doesn't look so emotionally 'heavy' and will also cover all eventualities – here's the how of it.

When to do it The best time is when you buy your home. When you are dealing with lots of other legal documents, drawing up a will may seem easier, believe it or not. Ask your solicitor to help you draw up a copy.

If you are not buying a home but do have a lot of savings or things of value, you can draw up your own will, although this is advisable only after a lot of homework. The Consumers' Association has several guides to will making and there are even some online solicitors who will charge you next to nothing.

What to do You need to decide who gets what, and you'll also have to agree on an executor – the person who will be in charge of distributing your assets when you die. This could be a family member or a close friend.

Who gets what if you have no will? If you don't make a will, you will die intestate. The laws of intestacy (covered by the Administration of Estates Act 1925) mean that your assets are divided up among the nearest relatives.

£   If you are married, your partner automatically gets personal chattels, such as furniture and jewellery, as well as £125,000. They also get a lifetime interest in half of what is left, such as an investment. Children, if there are any, automatically get half what is left if they are over eighteen. Stepchildren will not get anything.

£   If you have no children, your wife or husband gets the personal chattels, up to £200,000, and half of what is left. The other half is shared among parents, brothers and sisters.

£   If you have no partner, the children inherit all that is left after death duties.

£   If you have no partner or children, everything will pass to your parents, and if you have no parents it will go to your siblings. If you have no siblings it will go to half-brothers or half-sisters, or, in their absence, nieces and nephews. Next, it may go to grandparents, or to uncles and aunts (whole-blood brothers and sisters of your parents). If there are none of these it will go to half-uncles and -aunts (normally known as great-aunts or -uncles, or half-blood relatives). And, if there really is no one, all your assets will be passed to the state.

What if you're married? If you, or your loved one, die intestate, it is OK if there's only you and your partner involved, but things can get very complicated if one of you has children from a previous relationship, because, if no agreement is made, then children automatically inherit from their parent.

'My boyfriend has four children from a previous relationship,' says Joanne. 'We're planning to start a family but before we do so I'm going to make sure I get a will drawn up. I don't get on very well with his ex-partner, so I don't want his children being able to inherit my home. My will is going to make sure my sister, my brother, my mum, my children as well as my boyfriend, get something when I die.'

But I've got no one to leave it to Don't you believe it! Even parents have been known to fight over their children's worldly goods.

Sam's family were nearly torn apart after her oldest brother died in a car crash. 'He owned a couple of houses and wasn't married. In theory the cash went to my mother, my father and myself, being the only other sibling. Thing is, my parents were divorced and my brother hadn't seen my dad for several years. It got very, very messy because he hadn't made any will. Eventually, we had to go to court. My dad owed loads in debts and he wanted his hands on my brother's cash. He got some in the end. I really thought, My brother is going to turn in his grave. I just wish he'd sorted these things out when he bought his homes.'

SAME-SEX COUPLES – WHERE THE LAW STANDS

Having a living-together agreement is even more important than if you're an opposite-sex couple because the law still does not allow gay partners the same rights to each other's things as married couples. You may want to seek the advice of a specialist solicitor.

IF YOU ARE NOT MARRIED

Don't take it for granted that living together as a married couple will give you an automatic entitlement to your partner's share. You need to make sure you have something in writing. And, even if you are married, your share of things can be affected by the entitlement of a previous partner. There is no real legal definition of what is a common-law couple, although a lot of lawyers agree that if a couple have been living under the same roof for six months or more they become a 'common-law husband and wife'. The phrase 'common-law' in this context means that it's a generally agreed term, not one that has been set out by an Act of Parliament. Living together, however long, does not give either of you the same rights as being married.

GETTING MARRIED

With the abolition of the married couples' tax allowance, the most obvious *financial* reason for getting married has been all but removed.

There are a number of things that being married does change, however.

Your home If you already own a home together, then about the only financial thing that will change for you – if you are a woman, anyway – is the name that appears on your bank statement. This is because both your names will be on the deeds of the house. The deeds are the document that states who owns the property. This is normally kept by the solicitor who dealt with the house buying. If you are a woman you don't need to change your name on the deeds, even if you get married: a marriage certificate is proof enough.

If one of you owns the home you'll probably want to make sure that both of you are registered on the deeds of the house. This makes you joint owners of the family home. You do this by asking your solicitor to change the deeds; they will probably charge a fee for this.

'Somehow we never got round to putting my name on the deeds,' admits Johanna. 'When we got divorced it made an incredible difference to the legal settlement. We had quite an acrimonious split, so my lawyer had to use bank statements and savings books to prove that I had been paying my husband rent before we got married.'

Your will You will both still need to make a will, especially if either of you has children from a previous relationship or marriage. If either of you dies without making a will, you will be subject to the law concerning intestacy (see above).

Tax The married couples' tax allowance was abolished except for those born before 6 April 1935. If you have children and earn what is considered to be a low wage you may be entitled to a child tax credit, which will mean you pay a reduced rate of tax on what you do earn.

Pension – beware Always, always have your own pension. Even if you are not working you may still be able to stash your money into a retirement fund. The government has set up a second pension scheme for people who cannot work, such as carers or disabled people. Four years ago the law was changed to include pensions as an asset, and they could therefore be split in a divorce settlement. This meant that partners who haven't been paying into a pension – for example, full-time housewives or mothers – were given a right to part of their ex-partners' pension, but it's a lengthy legal process, so it's always best to have your own if possible.

WHEN THE WORST COMES TO THE WORST

You can try to make things work and protect yourself, but sometimes there isn't a lot more you can do. If you die without a will and you are married, your estate goes to your partner. If you are not married then your surviving family, as well as your partner, will be entitled to claim some of your cash. If any parents survive you they will also have a right to some of your money.

What if you've been helping your partner out with their mortgage? Claire, aged 38, says, 'I'd been living with my partner for fifteen years. We'd had an arrangement where I had paid him rent, and in return he had kept the house he'd bought before we'd been together. We ended up splitting up because I wanted kids and I wanted to get married. We'd bought a lot of stuff together and I had decorated the whole house during our time together. I'd also helped pay for a cooker and a fridge.

'When we split he let me take the fridge – big deal! Anyway, I'm not really very savvy but, during an evening out drinking with the girls, one of them, who works in a law firm, said she reckoned I may be entitled to a share of the house, because I'd been paying rent all that time. I had to go to my solicitor and I had to drag out all my statements, but in the end he ended up giving me a few thousand. I settled for that rather than a share of the house because he wasn't going to be selling for a while and I wanted a clean break.'

Clive, aged 56, says, 'It's been a very amicable split. We bought the house together but her parents put in a lot of the cash. I'm selling my part to her and getting around twenty thousand pounds, which I'll probably use as a deposit for another house.'

Lou, aged 42, says, 'It's been very messy. My husband died of cancer. He was my second husband and we hadn't been getting along for some while. In fact, when he was diagnosed with cancer, our relationship got worse. There were times when he told me he didn't love me any more. Anyway, he died and, just before, we did have a kind of resolution. Well, in his will things went to his first wife and his other children. I eventually got some settlement out of the will but I do wish that he had sorted it out before he died. It would have saved so much heartbreak.'

OTHER PROBLEMS

If money isn't the only thing blighting your relationship, it may be a good idea to get counselling. Contact your local Relate, or see your GP for a list of qualified psychologists.

If you need help getting tax and legal advice, see Chapters 6 and 7.

CHILDREN

Phew! You have only just sorted out your own finances and suddenly a bundle of joy appears. There is more information on your entitlements when you have children in **Your Working Life**.

AFFORDING CHILDREN

If you have been working for a while you are entitled to maternity pay. Some mothers can take a year off work and then go back to their old jobs. Maternity pay is not the same as being paid a full-time wage, though, and some mothers are often forced back to work (see **Your Working Life** for more information on maternity pay).

SAVING FOR YOUR YOUNGSTER

Because they are so young and don't pay tax you need put only the smallest amount away for your children. There are lots of children's bonds and baby bank accounts, and you can compare the rates of interest using the Moneyfacts website or doing a recce on the Internet.

GET MORE SAVINGS

If relatives insist on giving money as presents it may be a good idea to set up a savings account. Make a point of letting your youngster know that the money they do get is put into the account; even better, take them to the bank or building society so they can do it themselves.

'I've set up a savings account for my twins,' says Adele, 'and up to the age of two I was getting family members to give them money as a present. They want "proper" presents now, like dolls and Lego bricks, but I've managed to get them a good start. I now put in about twenty-five pounds a month.'

CAN I INVEST?

You can set up a share account in your youngster's name. These are more specialised savings and are not the same as ISAs – you have to be sixteen to open a cash ISA and eighteen to open a share ISA.

WHAT DO YOU TEACH YOUR KIDS ABOUT MONEY?

The value of money is something that very few of us can grasp ourselves, so how do we give our youngsters a healthy attitude to cash?

Setting pocket money 'Pocket money should be there to be used to encourage your kids to save and to spend,' says Ella. 'So you should give them enough to do both. This will help teach them that money is there to be enjoyed and not to be afraid of, it should not be locked away and never seen again for several years.

'You should make sure that youngsters do put a bit of their weekly money aside. To do that you need to teach them about the value of money. Giving them an idea of how much their beloved train set costs and how long it will take to save up for it will also teach them to budget.'

Giving money 'As a present, it is not always the best idea, but when it *is* sent that should be earmarked for saving,' Jacqui advises. 'Gifts should not just be money, as it will encourage greed, so you need to get a balance between buying a present and saving the money.'

Making them save 'Make taking them to the post office to put their money into a savings account an adventure,' says Lynda. Look for accounts that offer little extras, such as those NatWest piggy banks. Anything that makes saving a bit more fun. 'Oh, and let them keep their savings book and give them responsibility for it. Trusting your youngsters with money will send out good signals, too,' Lynda continues.

Teach them the value of money 'Don't bribe your youngsters with money,' says Ella. 'Make them work for it. But don't always offer money as an incentive – it will make them think that everything they do should be paid for. It's the last thing you should do. Money should not be a god. Very few people realise how much money should be respected. It's a means to an end, not an end in itself.'

WHEN YOU DIE

INHERITANCE TAX

You have heeded the advice and amassed all that cash. Well you've got to leave it to someone, haven't you? After you've thought about wills, here's a tax you need to know about, too – preferably *before* you die! It's called *inheritance tax*.

This tax has to be paid on things in your name – it could be a share of your home, your savings, your car. The good news is that the amount your estate has to be worth before your relatives have to start paying tax is £250,000 until April 2003.

You can escape having your beneficiaries pay inheritance tax if you gift expensive items, such as the house, *seven years* before you die. The Queen Mother did this with her grandchildren, to save them having to pay tax.

What cannot be taxed Even if you have given some large gifts within the seven years before you die you may still not have to pay tax. This would be wedding gifts, maintenance payments and other items worth less than £3,000 made in the previous tax year (the tax year starts on 6 April and ends on 5 April the following year).

How much gets taxed? The tax is a whopping 40 per cent, so anything over the £250,000 that is not exempt from inheritance tax will be taxed at 40 per cent.

How is it paid? It will either be your solicitor or the executor of your will who sorts out your tax bill.

CAPITAL GAINS TAX

Another tax that you may have to pay is capital gains tax. You may have to pay it on, for instance, a property that you inherited and then sell. The same applies if you sell some shares you inherit. Capital gains tax and how it works is explained more in **Your Working Life**.

5 A LITTLE BIT OF PROTECTION

Insurance makes us think of the very worst things in life: illness, death, fire, serious accidents, car crashes, storm damage, burglaries and loss of earnings. Sometimes we prefer *not* to think of them, but it's vital to have something in place to deal with the unexpected. The unexpected has a nasty habit of happening when you don't expect it, of course, so it's as well to draw comfort from the fact that you've done all you can to protect yourself and the people you love.

The best thing you can do is have enough ready cash to cope for the unexpected, but that's not always practicable or affordable.

In some cases, with cars and homes for example, having insurance is a necessity – with cars it's a legal requirement – but the idea of insuring most other things in life is often considered a luxury. There are, though, insurance policies that cover everything from your dog's dental work to your own life. Whether you need them or not is still a matter of debate – even financial advisers are not entirely agreed on what kinds of insurance we all need.

Of course, the devil of insurance policies is always in the detail, and one car-insurance plan may offer very different terms from another – so, if you do want to buy insurance, make sure you read that small print.

WHEN YOU LOSE YOUR JOB

Not everyone who is made redundant gets the financial cushion of a pay-off (check **Your Working Life** for your redundancy rights). If you're doing OK, now there are quite a few things you can do to make sure losing your job doesn't equal losing your lifestyle – not completely, anyway.

IF YOU'VE GOT A MORTGAGE AND A FAMILY

When there's much more than just yourself to think about, you need to give more thought to what happens if you lose your power to earn money. Here are some things you could set in motion.

Save Try to have about three to six months' salary stashed away to tide you over. This will allow major expenses such as mortgage repayments and bills to be kept up to date. Check **Saving** for ways of stashing your cash away.

Insurance When you take out a credit card, loan or mortgage you may be offered payment protection. These agreements pay out if you are suddenly out of work. There's lots of small print with these: some will pay out only when you've been out of work for more than six months; some may cover only part of payments; some will pay out for only a set amount of time.

Mortgage-payment protection These policies aren't cheap, and are normally calculated per £100 of your monthly mortgage repayments. A typical policy at the time of writing might require you to pay £5 per £100; so, if you've got a £600 monthly mortgage your mortgage-protection policy will cost £30 per month.

Note on loan, credit-card and mortgage-protection policies
Some insurance companies will ask you whether you want to be insured for 'any occupation'. This means that they may not pay out if you can get *any* kind of work, and not necessarily only that of your chosen trade or profession, or what you are qualified to do.

Mortgages that let you pay how much you want to You can take out a flexible mortgage plan – for more details see **Building a Nest**. These let you overpay, or underpay, so long as you make a minimum payment towards your mortgage each month.

Some people, like 28-year-old Imogen, a freelance reporter, found this handy. The precarious nature of her work meant a flexible mortgage was a good idea, but it soon became a better one. 'We had a flexible mortgage so when my partner and I were both earning we were putting quite a lot of our cash into getting the mortgage down,' she explains. 'Then I had a baby and we were only relying on one income. The overpayments came in handy because we could then "underpay" for a while, until I went back to work.'

IF YOU'RE RENTING

When you haven't got a mortgage losing your job isn't such a big deal, financially speaking. You can't take out an insurance policy to cover your rent but you can take one out to cover your credit cards or loans.

Saving Even when you are renting, it's still very useful for you to have savings. See **Saving**.

How do I pay my rent? If you have no choice but to carry on renting you may be entitled to housing benefit. This will depend on the savings you have, and your availability to work. If you have been paying National Insurance regularly (see **Your Working Life**) you'll be entitled to the full Jobseeker's Allowance. If you haven't you may get a reduced benefit known as income support. The latest benefit news can be found at your local job centre.

Kevin, a computer salesman from Lancaster, decided to keep paying rent. 'I lost my job about three years ago,' he says. 'I didn't get paid off, just a month tax-free. As soon as I knew my firm had started making people redundant I started looking around for other work. So when I knew I was being "let go" I decided to pay another month's rent and take a chance. I did get another job, down the road from my old place, so there was no need for me to tell my landlord.'

Simon, who lived in London when he lost his job, found paying rent too much. 'I got made redundant but my rent was way too expensive – six hundred pounds a month. I didn't have anyone to help share the bills, as I was on my own. I gave my notice in [on my flat] as soon as my firm told me my job had gone. I ended up having to move in with a cousin.'

Bear in mind that, if you do start to rely on state benefits to pay your rent, your landlord or letting agency may not be too happy, and may ask you to leave. If this happens, then they still have to give you notice, normally a month. Check your rental agreement, which should list exactly what happens. If it doesn't, then check with your landlord or rental agency on what would happen if you were to lose your job.

Why claiming benefit may still be a good idea Another reason to start claiming benefit is that you get your National Insurance contributions paid. NI contributions count towards your state pension.

What about bills? It's essential to let the electricity, gas and water companies know you're having trouble paying – very often they can work out a special budgeting plan while you're out of work.

Sara and her partner Sasha, both 33, didn't do this – to their own cost. 'I and my partner both worked in IT. We got made redundant within a couple of months of one another. Things went from very good – we had small payoffs – to bad. A year later we had amassed a thousand-pound electric bill we could not pay. In the end the electricity company put us on a meter where we had to prepay for our electricity and then at the same time the meter would gobble a certain amount to pay off what we owed, too. It was not ideal but it made budgeting the cash we did have that bit easier.'

PROTECTING YOURSELF IF YOU GET SICK

Your employer is legally entitled to keep paying you for up to 28 weeks if you are off sick, as long as you provide a doctor's note. Whether you get paid after 28 weeks will depend why you are off work: if it is a work-related accident or sickness, your employer may simply wait till you are recovered and keep paying you in the meantime.

If it's not a work-related sickness and you are going to be off work for a lot longer, you can either

£   claim benefit – statutory sick pay or incapacity benefit
£   claim on an insurance policy that you took out before you knew you were going to be sick

MEDICAL INSURANCE EXPLAINED

There are so many insurance policies covering sickness that it's easy to throw in the towel and dismiss them altogether. Most medical-related insurance is taken out in a subsidised package through work.

PRIVATE MEDICAL INSURANCE (PMI)

Private medical insurance covers the cost of medical treatment and may allow you to skip NHS waiting queues for nonessential surgery. It does not cover emergency treatment.

Lots of celebrities have private medical insurance because it means you have an easier time in hospital, you get a private room complete with all mod cons – think of Victoria Beckham when she had her baby Romeo.

Jacqui, aged 34, enjoyed her hospital stay. 'I had to have the toes on my feet broken and reset after an accident,' she explains. 'And I opted to go private. I had my own room and satellite television. I was only in for a couple of days and it was like being on holiday.'

PMI insurance companies include well-known names like BUPA and PPP. You can elect to include other cover, such as dental treatment, having a well-woman or well-man screening and even minor plastic surgery.

What you get depends how much you pay for. A lot of employers offer private medical insurance as a benefit, but you may still have to pay excess – that could be anything from £50 upwards.

Do I need a health check? It depends on the insurer. If you are doing it through your firm and you're relatively young you'll be automatically covered.

Are there things it doesn't pay out for? Yes, there are: private medical insurance varies from one insurer to another, so you should read all the print, large and small, and decide which is the best policy to suit your needs.

PERMANENT HEALTH INSURANCE (PHI) AND CRITICAL-ILLNESS COVER

PHI covers you if you get an illness that you're not likely to recover from, such as cancer or a stroke. It will cover costs of medical care but may not kick in until a few months have elapsed. It pays out an income, like a salary.

Critical-illness cover pays a tax-free lump sum (rather than an income) if you suffer from a major illness, known to insurers as a *critical illness*.

All critical-illness policies cover cancer. Most kinds cover heart attacks and strokes, but others may include other things, such as third-degree burns, Parkinson's disease and paralysis. Critical-illness cover is often included on life-insurance or mortgage-protection policies, so always check before you buy it.

Do I need it? If you live on your own, having either critical-illness cover or PHI means that you may not have to worry about paying the mortgage. It also means you can afford to pay for someone to look after you – this makes sense as more people opt to live on their own, and further away from their families.

What about cost? The younger you are the cheaper it is. As with private health insurance, you may get critical-illness cover or PHI through work.

Are all illnesses covered? Not all: some insurers will refuse to pay out if you take out a policy and then, say a month later, find out you have cancer. They could claim that you already knew you were sick when you took out the policy. This clause covers what is known as 'awareness of a pre-existing condition'. If someone is considered to be at risk from a certain disease such as AIDS, then an insurer can refuse to cover them in the first place.

Genetic testing With advances in science – think of the human genome project, which may enable doctors to pinpoint which diseases we're genetically disposed to – the question of genetic testing has reared its head. At the moment insurers will not *make* you take a genetic test, but, if you have had one in the past, they may want to see the results of it. As we went to press, this was still under discussion, but remember that this is an issue that will not go away. You can log on to the Association of British Insurers' website (www.abi.org.uk), which has details of a code of conduct for genetic testing.

PERSONAL ACCIDENT INSURANCE

When you read stories such as those about J Lo insuring her legs for £3 billion or Jonah Lomu insuring his biceps for £2 million, that's normally accident insurance. If you are self-employed, taking out accident insurance is more appropriate than if you are working for a firm.

If you have an accident at work, and it can be proved to be your firm's fault, you should be entitled to compensation. Under the Health and Safety at Work (Employer's Liability Compulsory Insurance Regulations 1998) Act, all firms must take out insurance to cover their employees should they suffer a work-related illness or accident.

If you have problems claiming that an accident at work was your firm's fault, contact your union or a specialist law firm. The Citizens' Advice Bureau will be able to help you if you are having problems finding a lawyer who specialises in claims.

PROTECTING YOUR THINGS

CAR INSURANCE

It's illegal to drive an uninsured car, but thousands of people still risk it; needless to say this is one expense you can't skimp on. Unfortunately, car insurers know that and getting inexpensive cover can take some shopping around. Thankfully, there are many insurance companies vying for business and the Internet has made getting a cheaper deal a lot easier. How much you pay and what kind of car insurance will depend on what you use your car for and how old it is.

With car insurance you'll pay either a monthly or an annual premium. If it's monthly and you make a claim on your insurance then you still have to keep paying your premium till the end of the twelve months – even if you are no longer using your car.

THIRD PARTY, FIRE AND THEFT

This is the most basic car insurance policy, and protects against just what it says it does. You get a pay out only if your car is stolen, set alight or involved in a crash with a third party. You don't normally get enough to cover the cost of the vehicle – that's why it's the cheapest of all. It's really intended to make sure that, if you are involved in a crash, the other driver is covered.

When should I go for this policy?

£   if your car isn't worth much – under £1,000, for example
£   if you are under 21, when taking out a fully comprehensive policy might be more expensive (some insurers will offer discounts if you are over 25, and in some cases over 35)
£   if you don't need your car for work

FULLY COMPREHENSIVE

This is the *crème de la crème* of car insurance. If you've bought a brand-new car, or you use your car for business, then fully comprehensive is the more expensive option. Cover will normally include replacement of the car if it gets written off (to its value when you bought it). You'll also get a courtesy car while your car is being fixed, breakdown cover and even free windscreen replacement. It will also cover you while you are driving someone else's car.

WHY DOES THE COST OF CAR INSURANCE VARY?

There are several reasons. Here are some of them.

£   Because of the value of your car: the more expensive it is, the more the insurer will need to pay you if you need to replace it
£   Because of where you live: if you live in a high-crime area, the chances that your car will be stolen increase
£   Because of your age: the younger you are, the more likely you are to have an accident
£   Because of your sex: women drivers are on the whole less likely to have an accident than men, so they tend to get cheaper insurance
£   How often you use the car: if you are working and use the car for more than just commuting, then you'll pay more, simply because you use the car more

CAN I REDUCE MY INSURANCE?

Taking an advanced driving course, a recognised one, is one drastic but great way of bringing down the cost of your insurance if you are under 21. But it's expensive and notoriously difficult to pass. You can live in a cheaper insurance area, buy a cheaper car and not use it for work. But if those options sound a bit drastic then your best bet is to shop around.

Insurers may reduce your premiums if you change employment: highly stressed occupations such as those of doctors, journalists and some city professionals attract higher premiums, while safer occupations, such as those of yoga teachers and acupuncturists, often attract cheaper insurance.

NO-CLAIMS BONUS

This is what you get if you don't use your insurance policy. If you don't claim on your insurance your premiums will gradually become cheaper. It also may be easier for you to switch to another insurance company.

A WORD ABOUT STUDENTS

One question students ask is whether it's worth taking their car to university. Before you go away, check how your insurer regards the area where you're going to study. Students moving to London might be advised to leave their cars at home, as the capital is one of the most expensive areas in the country. If you can't do without it, you should be insuring your car with a specialist student insurer. Check with your local National Union of Students branch – all the addresses are listed at the end of **Spending It**.

HAPPY HOLIDAYS

Holiday insurance will cover you for sickness – for flying you back home for medical treatment, for instance, or even getting you treated abroad. It will also pay out for lost luggage, lost cash, a stolen passport and even stolen jewellery.

Most holiday cover will have an excess of around £50 – this means that you have to cough up the first £50 of any claim, and the insurance company will pay for the rest.

What you get Some holiday insurance plans will cover you for up to £1 million; others will cover you for only a few thousand. The more cover you want, the more you have to pay. You can reduce your travel insurance costs by taking out an annual policy that even covers so-called dangerous sports such as skiing.

Can I skimp on it? You can travel without it, but if you're going on a sports-themed holiday – such as skiing – an insurance policy will cover you for any accident you may have. And you may just need it.

Mark, aged 22, and his daredevil mates from Surrey needed it. 'Two of us broke bones when we went skiing in Italy,' he says. 'It wasn't our first holiday skiing, so we were more foolhardy. I only broke my thumb, and ended up paying my medical costs and then claiming them back when I got home. This came to about two hundred pounds. My friend broke her thighbone – bad news, because she had to be stretchered off the piste. In the end she had to go home because her leg had to be in traction. We had taken out insurance and I think her costs were in the thousands. But it was all paid for.'

JEWELLERY, STEREOS, VIDEOS AND OTHER IMPORTANT THINGS

You can insure individual items in your home. You can get them covered for damage – if your home is flooded, say, or damaged by fire, or if you are burgled.

Kate, who has an eye for expensive jewellery, made sure she was covered. 'It's always best to keep the receipts of anything and try to buy anything expensive on a Visa card, because it's automatically insured,' she says. 'I've never had anything stolen but in the hurricane of 1987 we did have storm and flood damage, which claimed one of my watches. I was covered because I'd added it to my contents policy the week before.'

WHAT ELSE CAN AND CAN'T I INSURE IN MY HOME?

You can add cookers, stereos, computers, DVDs and even sofas. Some insurers also offer handbag insurance that covers valuables that are not always at home.

However, sometimes insurers may insist that you do certain work to make your home less likely to be burgled. Helena, aged 31, from south London, had to dig around to get her stuff insured. 'I was living in a shared house and the insurance company wouldn't touch my house with a bargepole – well not until we put into place bars in the windows, a mortise lock and locks on all the windows,' she says. 'We insisted the landlord do all this but he refused. In the end we went to a specialist insurance company that also insures students. It probably cost more but we couldn't afford not to insure it.'

HOW CAN I MAKE IT CHEAPER?

Some people move home to make their home and car insurance cheaper, but you can do some pretty simple things, such as making sure you've got a double lock, or even just a mortise lock.

Also worth installing is a burglar alarm or even burglar deterrents, such as a barking-dog recording or a light that flicks on when anyone comes within metres of the house. If you spend a lot of time at work it may be worth having a timed light that comes on when it gets dark. Remember: burglars are basically opportunists.

You could also install smoke alarms. Not only could this save you money on insurance, but it would also be a potentially life-saving precaution to take.

OTHER THINGS YOU CAN HAVE INSURED

Your home All homes – that's the building itself, not the contents (you have to take a separate cover for that, see above) – should be covered by buildings insurance. This will pay the cost of rebuilding your home should anything untoward happen to it. It doesn't reflect the amount you've paid for your home but what it will cost to rebuild it.

When you buy a freehold property – in other words, when you own the ground your house is built on – it will be up to you to make sure that buildings insurance is in place. If you are buying a leasehold property, normally a flat, it will be the landlord's responsibility to insure the building, but you may have to make a contribution towards it via maintenance charges (see **Building a Nest**).

Your pets Even sweet old Fido, Fluffy or Fifi can get the full Hollywood medical treatment nowadays. Pet insurance isn't too expensive, but it's still a luxury. If you are a real animal lover with a house to rival Doctor Doolittle's, then your veterinary expenses might benefit from an insurance policy. Otherwise, it may be worth thinking carefully before you buy.

Your wedding With more and more weddings costing more and more money, insurance companies are wising up to the cash to be made from making sure someone's special occasion doesn't cost too much because of unexpected hitches (if you'll pardon the pun). However, there are lots of conditions attached: some insurance policies will not cover bad weather, for example, while others may pay out if Hurricane Andrea or Zane decide to gatecrash your carefully planned marquee reception. It probably won't pay out, though, if one of you gets cold feet and calls the whole thing off.

'ACTS OF GOD'

Sometimes all the planning in the world can still leave you as high and dry as Noah's Ark on the top of Mount Everest. That's when the three words 'act of God' come in. This means that it is at the insurer's discretion as to whether they will cough up.

'My insurer refused to pay up because they say it was an "act of God" and it wasn't covered in my policy. I'm stuffed because I didn't read the small print,' says Roy, whose car was damaged by a slate from a neighbour's roof in a hurricane.

An 'act of God' – and you don't have to be a believer for these three words to appear on your insurance policy – is something like extreme weather or, more dramatic, a meteor crashing into your house. Different insurers have different ideas of what an 'act of God' is and sometimes they may still pay out, anyway.

Although flood could be considered an 'act of God', an insurer is more likely to cover it than, say, a satellite falling on a car. Hurricanes are still 'acts of God'.

'In New Zealand, when we buy a house, earthquake cover is added on automatically,' explained John.

WHEN ALL ELSE FAILS

If things get tough you can claim benefits from the government.
What you can claim depends on what savings you have, whether
you've got family you can get help from, or whether you have a
family of your own to support. There are many different kinds of
benefit and if you want more details you would be best off checking
either with your local Citizens' Advice Bureau or job centre.

These are just a few of the things you are, or may be, entitled to
claim:

- £ housing benefit, and, if you need it, a house to live in
- £ income support, which may cover any additional expense
- £ free prescriptions, dental care and eye tests
- £ Jobseeker's Allowance, although this will depend how long you have
  been working
- £ disability allowance that can cover the cost of having to make
  adjustments to your home
- £ widow's or widower's pension – whatever age you are
- £ Child tax credit – if you have youngsters

INSURING YOUR LIFE

You need life insurance if

- £ you've got children and you want to make sure they don't go without
- £ you've got a mortgage and you want it to be paid off should you die
- £ you want to leave your family something when you die

You *don't* need life cover if

- £ your pension or bank account includes it

WHEN LIFE INSURANCE ISN'T REALLY LIFE

There are two types of life insurance: *term*, which isn't really life
insurance at all because it covers you for only a fixed term –
normally 25 years, the same as the length of your mortgage; and
whole-of-life, for which you pay premiums monthly or yearly until
you either retire or die.

Some life-insurance policies say that they'll pay out 'cash if you die,
and cash if you don't' – these are more like savings accounts than
life insurance. They may have a life-insurance element, but

remember that, if you have savings, these are automatically paid out to your family anyway – unless you have made a will stating otherwise.

Incidentally, you'll hear of 'life insurance' and 'life assurance' – what's the difference? Well, none: they are the same thing.

WHOLE-OF-LIFE

With a whole-of-life policy your family automatically get cash when you exit the gene pool. You will agree the 'value' you want to insure your life for with an insurance company and will pay appropriate premiums. These will be invested by the life-insurance company on your behalf. You can choose to invest your premiums in what is known as a with-profits fund, which means you get a share of the profits the life-insurance company makes. These are paid into your fund on an annual basis and are often called bonuses.

TERM

Term assurance will give your family a lump sum of money that can be used to pay off outstanding bills or debts that they might no longer be able to afford. A lot of parents take out a term assurance policy when they take on a mortgage, so that they don't leave their family in the lurch. Often, they will set the term to expire when the mortgage is due to be paid off, so they are covered only for a specific length of time, hence the word 'term'. (A *terminal bonus*, incidentally, is not as ominous as it sounds: it is like a loyalty bonus that you get if you keep your life-insurance policy going for its full term).

A LIFE-INSURANCE ISA

The idea with a life-insurance ISA is that you can pay £1,000 a year into a policy tax-free, so the bonuses that you get don't incur any tax. (**Saving** looked at ISAs, so you may find it useful to go back and brush up.)

BUYING INSURANCE

Everything-but-life insurance General insurance, which is almost every type of insurance except life insurance, can be bought direct from an insurance company, or through a broker. It is not regulated but the companies that sell it are normally members of the Association of British Insurers. The ABI as it is known has a code of conduct that its members adhere to when they sell insurance. You can check details of the latest codes, including the one on genetic testing, through the ABI's website, or its helpline (both are listed at the end of the chapter).

When you buy insurance through the supermarket, such as Tesco's pet insurance, you are buying an insurance policy that is underwritten by a separate insurance company. The underwriter is the company that Tesco has paid to supply its customers with insurance and it is that insurance company that pays out when, or if, you make a claim.

A broker – you find brokers who sell on the Internet or through a shop – may be tied to several different insurance companies or may be independent, which means that they can sell the policies of all insurance companies and will be able to do a search for you to find the cheapest.

Brokers are paid via commission through the premiums that you pay the insurance company. The insurance company simply agree to pay the broker back a percentage of what you pay them. If you keep your policy going a long time, the broker can be paid what is known as *renewal commission*.

Brokers who sell whole-of-life insurance are regulated by the Financial Services Authority (FSA), because these policies also include an investment element. You'll see why this is necessary in **How (Maybe) to Make Pots More**.

INSURANCE DOS AND DON'TS

Here are some points that are definitely required reading, so consider them before you even *think* of buying insurance.

- £ Read the small print when you take out the policy.
- £ If you buy through a broker, check how much commission they are getting. This is important with long-term insurance such as life cover, because it could add hundreds of pounds to your premiums.
- £ With a medical insurance you may find that certain illnesses are not covered. Check which are and which aren't, and buy accordingly.

£   Pet insurance is a luxury, so don't expect it to be cheap.
£   Life insurance is often included as an extra on other financial products, such as mortgages and pensions.
£   Try to save into an ISA so you always have some cash available.
£   If all else fails, claim benefits.

INSURANCE HELP

If your insurance company goes belly up then you may be entitled to a refund of premiums.

The **General Insurance Standards Council** ensures that insurance companies abide by a code of standards, whether they are selling through high street store or on the Web.

The **Association of British Insurers**, or ABI, produces lots of free information covering all sorts of insurance. You can get this via their website on www.abi.org.uk or by phoning 020 7600 3333.

The **Insurance Ombudsman Bureau** – 135 Park Street, London SE1 9EA – can help if you feel your claim has been wrongly turned down. The enquiry line is on 0845 600 6666. Check the website on www.theiob.org.uk.

If you need to contact your local **Citizens' Advice Bureau**, see **Money and Relationships**. They can help you with information about state benefits and legal claims you may need to make.

6 YOUR WORKING LIFE

The last few chapters have told you how to spend it, to save it and even what to do with it when you die. Now it's time to look at how to get it in the first place.

WORKING FOR A LIFETIME

Although the British spend more time actually at work – they spend more time in the workplace than in any other country apart from the USA, and that's because Americans get less holiday time – they spend less time working for the same company than their parents or grandparents did. The job for life, where you started working for a firm at sixteen and stayed there right through till you swapped the suit for a pint and a pipe and slippers is no longer.

People are also getting more choosy about *what* they do to earn their money. It's unlikely that you haven't heard of someone who has switched career, or 'downsized' – taken a pay cut and slashed their working hours so they can take time out to travel, hang out with their family or take up a hobby or interest they have always wanted to do.

David was an insurance salesman for years until he jacked it all in to do up his house. Then in his early fifties he decided to pursue what he had always wanted: to be a guitar teacher. He's paid off his mortgage and is doing what he always wanted.

Those in their mid-thirties are choosing to switch their jobs, too. Many of us are dumping supposedly rewarding careers to follow our dreams.

Louise had already had two careers by the age of 36. 'I started off working as a journalist,' she says, 'and did that for eight years before I realised that I wasn't cut out for the selling your granny down the river. So I retrained by taking a textile course and learning to be a fashion designer.'

Employers and banks are slowly wising up to our work-more-and-play-harder lifestyles. Slowly and surely, our bosses are getting more flexible about the hours that we put in, and banks are bringing out products, such as flexible mortgages, that fit around our needs.

But that doesn't mean every boss is quite so accommodating, so it's important to wise up on your rights if you are planning on taking time out.

EARNING A LIVING

In case you don't already know, here are the basics you should be aware of.

How much should I be earning? Everyone over the age of eighteen is entitled to earn a minimum wage of £3.60 per hour; if you are 22 or over this is £4.20.

What should I be paying? Before you even get your salary, two chunks are taken out: the smaller one is your National Insurance contributions (NICs); the larger one is what you pay in tax. Both bits are taken by different government departments in order to fund public services, such as health, education and benefits. What you pay in NICs and tax is changed each year by the Chancellor of the Exchequer during the budget.

Not everyone pays the same rate of tax: it depends how much you earn and whether you are entitled to tax credits. Tax credits are payments given back to you by the Inland Revenue and will be paid if you have one or more children and work at least sixteen hours a week. You get a basic credit of £59 per week and then a thirty-hour credit of an additional £11.45 if you work thirty hours or more a week. You may get more if you have a disabled child or are yourself disabled.

National Insurance contributions The rate of National Insurance you pay depends on your salary and, like tax, is set each year. If you are in full-time employment – not just on a fixed-term contract – National Insurance will automatically be deducted from your wages. If you are self-employed it will be up to you to make sure you keep up your NICs. You can do this by contacting your local social security office, also known as the Department of Work and Pensions (the telephone number will be in your local telephone directory under Job Centres). It's important to try to keep up your NICs because making regular payments means you will be entitled to benefits including:

£ **incapacity benefit**
£ **Jobseeker's Allowance**
£ **maternity allowance**
£ **retirement pension (there's more about this in Building a Nest)**
£ **widowed mother's allowance**
£ **widow's payment**
£ **widow's pension**

TAX

How much am I taxed? You can earn up to £4,615 before paying tax in the tax year 2003/2004. This is your personal allowance and, despite its name, it is the same for everyone.

If you earn more than that, you start paying more tax. If you earn up to £1,920 above the £4,615 personal allowance, you pay 10 per cent tax. So you'll pay only 10 per cent of any amount between £4,616 and £6,535.

What if I earn even more? If you get above £6,535, you go into the 22 per cent tax range. And when you start to earn above £29,900 you then pay 40 per cent tax – but remember that you still have to take into account your personal tax-free allowance, so really you don't start paying top-rate tax until you earn £29,901 plus the £4,615, so you pay only 40 per cent tax on any amount over £34,515. If you earn £34,615 you'll pay 40 per cent tax only on the extra £100 and the rest (minus, of course, the allowance) will be taxed at 22 per cent.

'When I first started working I had a Saturday job at Marks & Spencer,' says Louise. 'I didn't pay tax on anything for a year because I earned below the allowance. When I started to earn better money – eleven thousand pounds – I paid around two thousand five hundred pounds in tax.'

So, if you earn £6,000, only £1,385 is taxable, and that will be taxed at 10 per cent, leaving you to pay tax of £138.50. There are still exceptions to the tax rules: self-employed people can claim back other taxes they have paid, such as value-added tax (VAT).

Don't married people get special benefits? No, they don't: the married couple's tax allowance was scrapped for all married couples born after 1935.

Can I get any tax back? If you give up work to go back to being a full-time student then you can also claim back some of the tax you paid. Students may not have to pay tax if they work during their summer holidays if they earn below their allowance.

Tax rebate – hot off the press At the time of writing, the government may be about to scrap a rule that allows top-rate taxpayers to pay a larger tax-free percentage of their wages into their pension. At the moment people paying the top rate of tax can put more cash into their pensions because they get a 40 per cent rebate rather than just a 22 per cent one.

MORE ON TAX

There are many different types of tax, but the most important one you need to know about if you are working is income tax. Other taxes you pay are VAT, which is added to most things you buy. There's also stamp duty, which is the tax you pay when you buy a house worth over £60,000. Then there is inheritance tax (see **Money and Relationships**) and capital gains tax, which normally applies only to things such as businesses and investments.

How is tax taken away? If you get your salary through an employer, your tax is deducted from your pay packet through a system called *Pay As You Earn* (PAYE). If you are self-employed, you have to work out your own tax once a year by filling in a self-assessment form.

Self-assessment was introduced in 1997 and enables people to work out their own tax. If that sounds frightening you can get an accountant to do it for you. You can fill your return in online (www.inlandrevenue.gov.uk) or you can order a form by calling the Inland Revenue's tax hotline (listed in **Resources**, with a lot of other useful contact information).

When do I have to work out my tax? You normally have to hand in the form by the end of September if you want the Inland Revenue to calculate your tax for you. If you are paying an accountant to calculate your tax then it doesn't have to be in until the January after the end of that tax year. So, if you are doing a tax return for the tax year April 2002 to April 2003 and you want to work out your own tax, or you are paying someone to do it, then you don't have to hand in your return until 31 January 2004.

When might I still have to do my own tax? It's not just self-employed people who have to fill in self-assessment forms. People who pay into pensions and pay 40 per cent tax may have to fill in a self-assessment form to make sure they get their pension tax rebate. People who own a lot of shares also have to fill in a self-assessment form, because the money shares generate is also taxable.

'I'd had a really bad year workwise and gave it up to concentrate on starting a florist's business,' says Sara. 'I had to fill in a self-assessment form and because I'd hardly earned anything I ended up actually getting money from the taxman. That was pretty good!'

You may also have to fill in a tax return if ...

£   you get extra income from renting out a house you own
£   you earn other income from investments (not including ISAs) – this includes dividends, the money you earn each year from shares

Getting an accountant to help you with your first tax return can make things seem less scary and can save you money.

'Each year I buy a laptop,' continues Sara, 'but it wasn't till I got an accountant to do my tax return that I realised I could actually register for VAT and get the VAT I'd paid on it back. I've set up a gardening business and I also found that I could claim back a lot of the expenses I'd forked out – excuse the pun – on garden implements.'

Capital gains tax (CGT) This is a tax you pay in addition to income tax, but you'll pay it only if you sell a sizable asset. To pay CGT you have to have made what the Inland Revenue reckons is a *chargeable gain*, meaning that something is worth more when you sold it than it was when you bought it.

Capital gains tax is based on what you make in a year, like income tax. There is a personal allowance, as with income tax, that you can make before you start paying CGT, and that is £7,500.

CGT can be paid on

£ **shares (see How (Maybe) to Make Pots More)**
£ **unit trusts**
£ **land and buildings, including rent from a house you own**
£ **business assets**

It doesn't get paid on

£ **a private car**
£ **personal belongings worth £6,000 or less**
£ **cash or foreign money**
£ **savings certificates and UK government gilts or bonds**
£ **shares in a venture-capital trust**
£ **shares in an approved share-option plan (see below)**
£ **money in an ISA or a PEP**

Even if you give things away to avoid death duties (see **Money and Relationships** for Inheritance tax), you will still have to pay tax on any capital gain on it (CGT).

If you are unsure about CGT, you should seek advice from a tax expert. The calculations used to work out CGT payments can be complex.

What you should do Keep a note of everything you spend your money on in that particular tax year. If you do leave paid employment make sure you keep your P45. You should also make sure you include your P60, which is the form that the Inland Revenue sends you once a year, normally at the end of the tax year, to say how much tax you have paid via PAYE.

'I made sure I kept all my food receipts, as well as the stationery and phone bills,' says Sara. 'And I made it clear which ones were work-related.'

If you have your own business or are a self-employed contractor the Inland Revenue also expect you to:

£ **Record all receipts as they come in as well as all the things you buy.**
£ **Keep backups – for example, make sure you keep copies of invoices, bank statements and paying-in slips.**
£ **Make a note of amounts taken out of a business bank account, or in cash, for your personal use.**
£ **Keep track of personal things – all amounts paid into the business from**

personal funds: for example, the proceeds of a life-insurance policy or
even investments.

Tax-free cash Investing your money in an ISA can help some of
your cash escape the ravages of the taxman, but did you know that
if you give money to charity the charity can claim back all the tax
you pay? That means that, even if *you* don't get it back, someone
else, other than the taxman, will benefit from your generosity. This
is known as *gift aid*.

HOURS OF WORK

If you're working for yourself you can pretty much choose the hours
you want to work, within reason, of course. But if you are working
for a firm then there are rules to make sure you don't have to
spend your days propping up your eyes with matchsticks.

The European Union has come to the rescue of clock watchers
everywhere with its Time Directive. This means that we don't have
to work more than 48 hours a week if we don't want to. That may
sound like a long week but, if you often put in more hours than you
strictly ought, you should have been asked to sign a waiver that
tells your boss you don't mind putting more hours in if you have to.

Whether you get paid extra cash for working longer hours depends
on whom you are working for. A temp or a contractor who gets paid
by the hour may simply get their hourly rate while someone
working as staff may be entitled to time off in lieu rather than extra
cash. These kinds of detail will be in any employment contract that
you have signed.

David, aged 23, who lives in Plymouth, said, 'Working on a local
newspaper, we had a rota of who worked the bank holidays. Well,
news doesn't just stop then, does it? If we worked a bank holiday
we would get a day off instead, which when you think about it is
almost as cool because we could take a day off midweek.'

OVERTIME INTO OVERDRIVE

With some jobs, it's taken as read that you'll put in all the hours
you can. Lawyers and doctors often make their way up the career

ladder by putting in extra time – and then some. Remember, though, that working lots of extra time may win you brownie points with your boss in the short term, but is not that great for your health.

'I worked on several major projects,' says Simon. 'All involved very long evenings when I hardly saw my partner. After six months of working like this, with no holiday, I started getting sick, and eventually had to be told by the doctor not to go into work.'

HOLIDAYS

If you work for a company, you should get days off and holiday, but these vary wildly from firm to firm. Under EU law, temporary staff who have been working full-time are also entitled to build up holiday, or at the least holiday pay. This means you shouldn't have to go without.

PERKS OF THE JOB

Slogging your guts out for a company should carry with it some financial rewards, not just the once-a-year chance to kiss someone you fancy under the mistletoe at the Christmas party. Here are some of the benefits you might get.

SABBATICALS

This is like a holiday, but much, much better. In this transient world, where even a year can seem a long time to be working for the same company, some firms reward their most loyal staff with a period of paid – yes, paid – extended leave.

Jason, a managing editor with a construction magazine, enjoyed a three-month sabbatical after working for the same company for five years. 'I got time to decorate the house, travel a bit,' he says. 'I saw relatives in America and I visited old mates. I even proposed to my girlfriend. Having those three months off work was one of the best things that happened to me.'

But taking time out can also leave you feeling restless. Jason continues, 'I got back to work and some of the people who I'd managed had moved on to more senior roles. I realised that I didn't want to be working there still. So I ended up going to the US and working out there.'

So taking a few months or a year off can give your career a kick-start or it can make you rethink the whole rat-race thing.

It wasn't Kat's company's policy to let staff have sabbaticals but she asked anyway. 'After working for ten years I felt needed a year off to travel. I rented out my flat, sorted out all my finances and took off. I came back a year later and decided to work for a charity. I'd been working in media sales and realised that I wanted to put something back.'

If you do want to go on a sabbatical make sure that:

£   **your boss gives you a written agreement**
£   **you can afford it – not all sabbaticals are paid**
£   **you really do need a break – or are you just seeking to escape problems that might be better dealt with by staying put, and how would you feel if, like Jason, you missed out on a promotion?**

FLEXIBLE WORKING HOURS

You don't have to be a megabucks entrepreneur to work the hours you want *when* you want, but an understanding boss most certainly helps. For years public-service employees, such as civil servants and council workers, have been able to take advantage of flexitime. This is a system that, though there are rules, gives them relative freedom to work the hours they want, so long as they work a certain number of hours a month. By putting in extra time over a number of days or weeks, workers can save up for days off.

Most people don't work in such an enlightened workplace, but from April 2003 employees have the right to ask for more flexible working hours. As it stands at the moment, these new rules apply only to workers with a family, and you have to prove that the reason you want to change your hours is because you need the time off for childcare. It works a bit like this:

£   **You ask your boss if they will think about your request; you have to have a child under six; and you have to have been working for your firm for at least 26 weeks.**

£   They then have 28 days to mull over it and then 14 days when they have to meet you to tell you their decision.

Of course your boss could refuse, but they have to have good reasons for doing so. They could say:

£   It will cause poor work performance. If you are a credit controller chasing debts, for example, then it might be necessary for you to work nine till five because those are the normal hours of the businesses you are dealing with.
£   They can't cover for you. If you are in a small firm there might not be anyone to cover for you.

You can go to an employment tribunal if you feel your boss is being unfair. If the tribunal thinks you have a case it may even award you monetary compensation.

SHARE OPTIONS

One way of encouraging staff to work harder is to give them a stake in the company they work for. If a company is listed on the stock market (see **How (Maybe) to Make Pots More**) it can do this by allowing its employees to buy shares.

A share option is not an actual share but the chance to buy a share at a special set price. Some companies give you share options while others will make you pay into a share-option scheme. Some share-option schemes will mean that you have to pay a certain amount into a savings account and this is called *Save As You Earn* (SAYE).

With an SAYE scheme you pay in a small or large amount – some start at around £25 and let you put in as much as £250. This normally comes straight out of your salary. When you start paying into the scheme you'll also be told how much you will be allowed to buy the shares at; this is called the *option price*.

Slowly, you build up a pot of money that is then used – at a time decided by your company – to buy shares at the set price. But you don't have to buy the shares at that time if you feel they are a bad buy.

Samuel joined his firm's share-option scheme. 'I'd been paying into a share-option scheme that allowed me to buy shares at five pounds,' he says. 'I'd been saving twenty-five pounds a month. Then the exercise period came up [when he was allowed to sell them] but the shares were actually selling for four pounds, so I decided to leave it another year before I bought the shares. A year later they were worth ten pounds, so I made five pounds on each share.'

Other share-option schemes might not need you to *buy* shares at all. With these schemes your firm *gives* you shares.

'I was given two thousand shares at an option price of three pounds fifty. When the time came for me to cash in my options the price of the shares was four pounds. What I got was the profit, not the full price of the shares. My shares were worth eight thousand pounds, but what I got was fifty pence from each share, so I ended up making a thousand pounds. That had to be taxed at twenty-two per cent, so in the end I got closer to seven hundred pounds.'

Beware of share options Fledgling firms such as dotcoms and IT businesses have used share options as a way of luring people out of fairly secure jobs into less secure ones. The idea of share options sounds great: you get paid £20,000 but you get £20,000 worth of share options. The value of shares, as we have seen, can go down as well as up. Think of them as an added potential, not as a sure thing.

PROFIT SHARING

If a company is not listed on the stock market it can still offer its employees a similar arrangement. But, instead of buying shares in the company, you may be asked to join a profit-sharing scheme, the percentage of which will probably depend on how long you have been working for the firm. If the company you are working for is a limited company – owned by private shareholders rather than stock market investors – but has plans to list on the stock market, you may be offered a share agreement, whereby you'll be given a certain number of shares when the company floats (this is explained more fully in **How (Maybe) to Make Pots More**).

SEASON-TICKET LOAN

Not perhaps as lucrative as being able to buy shares, but being able to buy an annual rail or bus ticket can save you a bit of cash on travelling to work. When you get a season-ticket loan it will normally be interest-free, and for that your firm is allowing you to pay up front for your annual travel costs, but allowing you to budget monthly, as that's when the loan is deducted straight from your pay packet.

'You end up getting about two months free than if you had kept paying per week or per month,' reckons Melanie. 'With some season tickets you get a reduction when you travel at weekends. I travel out to Liverpool Street at the weekends and they give me a third off my other travel.'

TRAVEL ALLOWANCE

There are some firms who will actually pay, yes pay, for some of your travel, especially if you have to spend a lot of time on public transport. 'I work for a firm of surveyors and property researchers,' says Helen. We get an annual travel card that allows us to travel round the centre of Manchester.'

'I worked as a newspaper reporter in northwest London,' says Dave. 'Our firm reimbursed us the cost of a weekly travel card. It was only around seven pounds at the time but when you're only earning about nine thousand pounds a year getting that cash was sometimes the only way we could afford to go down the pub.'

COMPANY CAR

Having a car is an incredible perk – but an expensive one for you. How much you get taxed on it depends on how much you use it, so if your car is essential to your job it may actually work out cheaper to buy one using a loan or to see if your firm will let you buy your company car.

GYM MEMBERSHIP

Gyms love companies who join en masse. They get a lot of new members and you get a special deal. Some gyms will waive your joining fee, and then charge you a reduced monthly subscription.

Others will charge you a nominal joining fee and a reduced monthly subscription.

Joining a gym is worth it only if you are actually going to bother to go there in the first place. Thousands of pounds are wasted every year by people who join gyms and then never bother to go, as Tanya, a gym receptionist, moaned. 'One guy turned up about a year after he last came in for a workout and wondered why his stuff had been taken out of the locker. He'd been paying sixty pounds a month for a year and hadn't even used the gym.'

Just because you are not full-time staff doesn't mean you cannot have your share of office perks, like joining a gym.

HEALTH INSURANCE

Some companies offer health insurance free to their high-flying execs, although it may still count as a taxable perk.

If you're working for a medium to large firm you may be offered the choice of joining a whole host of health-related policies (see **A Little Bit of Protection** for more details). If you already have health cover, check whether or not it will be cheaper to swap to the policy your firm is offering. If you are with the same company you may be able to swap your monthly premiums over. But you have to ask.

James, an IT contractor, swapped his accident insurance for a cheaper policy when he started a permanent job, and saved money. 'I had taken out personal accident insurance because I was self-employed,' he says. 'When I took a job at a firm I noticed that they were offering me cover with the same firm I had the private policy with. My wife got in contact with them and asked them if I could swap over but keep the fund going and they let me.'

PENSION WITH LIFE INSURANCE

When you join your company scheme look carefully at the booklet you get. Nearly all private company schemes, excluding stakeholder schemes, will include a life-insurance cover as part of the pension package. This means if you die your family will get a lump sum of money from your pension fund. The amount varies but is normally based on a percentage of your salary.

NOT PERKS, BUT NECESSITIES

So much for the perquisites. However, there are some things that you are, by law, entitled to.

IN SICKNESS AND IN HEALTH

We all become ill, but sometimes that sniffle that's been caught by everyone from Bert in accounts to Sheila in reception can turn into something that leaves you feeling poorly for more than a few days.

What happens when I'm off sick for a long time? You can have as much sick leave as you need – whether you get paid for all of it is another matter. Most firms will require you to have a signed doctor's note if you are off work for more than six working days. They may need this to show to their insurer because firms take out insurance themselves to cover themselves against too much sick leave.

Operations, routine or emergency, count as sick leave and you should still get paid, although not all companies are generous.

'They docked my pay,' says Linda. 'You were allowed five sick days a year. And if you worked for six months and you were left, in April, having had three days off since January, they would dock half a day off your pay because you'd taken more than your pro-rated amount.'

What happens when it's more serious If you are pretty sick and you won't be going back for a while – your firm can do several things. It can keep paying you, or it can put you on sick pay, which may be a reduced amount of your salary. If you've taken out a medical policy it may be time to get your claim in.

You can't be sacked for being sick but if you have taken unreasonable amounts of time off work without producing a doctor's note or evidence of your illness your pay may be docked.

Accidents will happen What if you aren't sick but you still have to take time off work for other issues, such as family concerns or an accident? Well, if it can be proved to be your fault, a minimum sick-leave allowance may be the most you can expect. People sometimes end up suing their employer because they've had an accident at work.

Kay watched one of her colleagues have an accident in the office-stationery firm where they worked. 'Sarah was rushing about. It was a deadline for a very important project. She dashed down the stairs and ended up falling on some wet stairs. There was a yellow sign up warning us the stairs were being cleaned but she claimed she hadn't seen it. She broke her leg quite badly and insisted on going to a solicitor. In the end she got nothing because she simply had been too busy rushing around.'

If you work with chemicals or other substances that could be considered dangerous if inhaled, touched or even seen, then your company is under a legal obligation to make sure that you are trained to deal with potential hazards.

PENSION

All firms with more than five employees have to provide a stakeholder pension for their workers. They don't have to add to it. **Getting Old** deals with pensions in detail.

BABY TIME

Having a baby doesn't mean you should be out of pocket. Firms have to allow new mothers and fathers time off to enjoy with their offspring.

MAN'S WORK

Thankfully, most firms and the government realise that men want to take as much responsibility for looking after their kids as women do. The government is looking at increasing the rights of fathers to take more paternity leave – they currently get only a week.

Paul, a chartered surveyor and new and dutiful father, took his time and a bit more. 'I took my week and then two more,' he says. 'The surveyor's firm where I work is quite small and my boss is quite good with letting us have leave because he has two small children himself. I didn't get paid the two extra weeks I took off, but I was allowed them.'

MOTHERS' RIGHTS

All pregnant women are allowed to take eighteen weeks of what is called *ordinary maternity leave*, but you don't have to get paid unless you have been working somewhere for a year – and that year end must fall on the eleventh week before the baby is born. So, to put it simply, you have to be in a job for at least seven months before you get pregnant.

By the way, all kinds of maternity leave, paid or not, mean that your employer has to keep your job open for you. Whether or not you get paid depends on lots of things, but we'll come to those.

What you get with ordinary maternity leave During those eighteen weeks you are still considered employed and you will continue to build up your holiday. In fact you get everything you would normally get if you were still working. If you are in a share scheme or have health club membership you will still benefit from those schemes, too.

But here's the rub: if you have been working there less than a year, you are not entitled to get paid. Of course, firms are different, and some may still pay you regardless. If you are unsure of your firm's policy on maternity leave then you either need to speak to your personnel manager, or check your employment contract.

The pay bit If you have been working *more* than a year, you get *statutory maternity pay* (SMP). This works out at 90 per cent of your salary for the first six weeks and £75 a week for the rest of the twelve weeks. Again, you may get more, because some firms are more generous than others when it comes to maternity rights.

If you are not entitled to SMP you can claim eighteen weeks' worth of *maternity allowance* (MA) from the government, which works out at £75 a week, but you have to have been in a job in the first place. If you haven't, you may still get incapacity benefit.

New mothers who have been working for their firms a year or more get leave – again, whether it is paid or not depends on the boss. This *additional maternity leave* allows you to take 29 weeks' leave starting from the week the baby is born (at which point your SMP comes to an end). You still get 29 weeks even if you have taken some of your 18 weeks' ordinary leave. If you do get paid during the additional bit, and then you don't return to work, you may have to repay some of the cash.

When the baby is born All new mothers get two weeks off after the baby is born and four weeks if they work in a factory. There are some jobs in which you may not need to go back to work till much later, no matter how long you have been working for the firm. This is more appropriate for young mothers who are working with chemicals.

Tell the boss Make sure you give your boss good notice, by law you have to let them know that you need maternity leave at least 21 days before you intend to take it. It may be a good idea to let your boss know before your bump starts showing.

When your baby is born you need to let your boss know, and you also have to give them 21 days notice before you go back to work.

Other time-off entitlements You are also entitled to time off in order to go to appointments for antenatal care. Your time off doesn't have to include only medical checkups: it could also include relaxation, breathing and even parentcraft classes. Make sure you have your appointment card or a certificate from your midwife to show to your boss as well.

CAN MY FIRM SACK ME IF I GET PREGNANT?

No, they can't. The only way you can lose your job is if you are made redundant while on leave or if your company closes down. However, there are some grey areas when it comes to maternity leave, as Josephine found out. 'There were quite a few redundancies made in the week before I'd told my boss I was pregnant. Myself, who was four months pregnant – and another mate who was also pregnant – was among the redundancies. Thing is, we could never really prove anything because our jobs were being made redundant, but I'm convinced that they got rid of us because we were pregnant.'

What can I do if I have been treated unfairly? Being a member of a union helps, because you get free legal advice. If you are not a member of a union you may be able to get specialist legal help through your local Citizens' Advice Bureau.

LOSING YOUR JOB

Chapters 2 (**Debt: The Good the Bad and the Ugly**) and 5 (**A Little Bit of Protection**) covered some of the basics of losing your job. Just to recap, though, what's the difference between being made redundant and being sacked?

£   **Redundancy. Being made redundant is when your job is no longer necessary, or other people can work around it. However, a lot of redundancies are made because the company is in financial difficulty or needs to cut down on its staffing bill.**

£   **Being sacked. You don't normally get a payout. To sack staff a firm has to prove that they have been bad employees – and that doesn't just mean turning up late every day with a hangover. If you are doing your job well, you won't get sacked.**

How can you get the better of your boss when it comes to losing your job? You may think your job is secure, and that they'd have you working there for life. But remember: no one is indispensable.

£   **Make sure your notice period is as long as possible – if you do get another job, you can always negotiate a shorter period, but if you are made redundant you'll get paid whatever.**

£   **Keep a written record of everything you send to your manager: every time you ask for holiday leave, when you take sick leave and when you ask for help with your workload.**

£   **If you manage staff, keep records of all appraisals you have with them. If they ask for holiday leave or are in charge of certain projects make sure that you have written evidence to back it up.**

GETTING MORE

What if you've been working at your job for, say, two years and there's no sign of a wage rise? You need to ask yourself if you were promised regular wage rises when you started. Check your contract or your job-offer letter before you go to your boss demanding money. If you were promised a rise, then you need to ask why you haven't got it. They might give you replies like these:

'We have no money to give you' Then you ask them when they will. If it looks unlikely, you have to do some deep soul-searching and ask yourself if you want to keep working for a firm that does not value its staff enough to reward them with more pay.

'You need to pull your socks up' You need to ask your boss what they expect of you and for them to put that down in writing. After that, get your boss to give you a performance checklist with the things they expect and how long they expect you to take. Then make sure that they promise that they will give you a rise if you meet their criteria.

'I wasn't meeting my deadlines,' admits Steve, 'nor was I organised with my paperwork, so I got my supervisor to give me a timeframe of six months in which to sort myself out. I vowed to get it done, and then to ask for a pay rise.'

Ask if there's any room for achieving some things and simply making progress on others. 'I was told I had to carry out more staff appraisals,' Joe says. 'So I did all the team, even though some of them had been seen fairly recently. I also got more organised with my paperwork. My boss still tried to wheedle out of it but I was insistent that I'd made the changes he wanted. In the end he had to offer me a rise.'

GOING YOUR OWN WAY

Becoming self-made is one way out of the rat race, but it takes guts, imagination and a good business brain to go there. Oh, and some of our advice as well.

Are you ready for it? Do you have a passion that you could turn into a living? A musical talent, a love of cooking, a way with words and a feel that you could do things better? These are all good starting blocks for your sprint away from the rat race. And forget age: it's never too late to turn your love of something into a money-spinner.

'I'm nearly sixty,' says David. 'I used to be an insurance salesman but when I came into my late forties I'd had enough. I was depressed and wondered where my life was going. I had a family who had grown up and I wanted to do something for myself. So I decided to take a musical teaching course. I'd been playing the guitar for thirty-odd years and that was my starting point.'

COULD YOU GO IT ALONE?

If you have a skill that everyone wants a piece of, you don't have to set yourself up in business to go it completely alone. Sasha, a translator, was made redundant from a large City law firm, but along the way she'd managed to impress a few contacts. 'I found that I was able to work as a contractor. So I had regular work, but variety.'

Being self-made is about having the confidence to carry a great idea through, but you also need to have the cash to do it. Here's where you can go next.

Banks and building societies Banks and building societies have small-business sections especially designed to help people wanting to go it alone. You'll be expected to come up with a business plan and an idea of how much money you'll need. Like students, new businesses often get special loan-repayment deals that allow you a cheaper rate of interest during those cash-precious early years.

Venture capitalists These are stock-market-listed companies whose sole business is to invest in fledgling companies. They will normally insist on a share of your profits and will also want to have some say in how the business is run. If the idea is successful they might even help your business achieve a full stock-market listing.

'I worked for a magazine company run by venture capitalists,' says Claire, 'but they weren't interested in the staff at all. They basically ran the company like a moneymaking shell. But in the end they sold us for a heck of a lot of money. We're now run by a management buyout team and they are far more interested in looking after staff development. Saying that, the venture capitalists helped keep the company going and gave it a continued profile.'

Private finance You can raise the money yourself. This means approaching people who will be interested in your idea. This could be wealthy relatives, friends who've got cash to spare and even local businesspeople.

Raising cash this way is trickier, since it's you who have to do all the footwork. Getting relatives involved can be a good and a bad thing: if the business fails you may end up owing money to your entire family.

MAKING SURE YOUR IDEA STAYS YOUR IDEA

If you are inventing something that you believe no one has ever thought of, make sure your idea is protected so that no one else can steal it. You can do this by copyrighting it, or patenting it. The Patent Office in London (details are at the end of the chapter) has a helpline that talks you through legal details.

USEFUL ADDRESSES

If you want to sort out your tax or set up your own business, you'll need to sort yourself out with an accountant. Here are some useful addresses for you.

The Institute of Chartered Accountants in England and Wales is a pretty good place to start. They have regional offices that can put you in touch with a local tax expert. Contact them on 020 7920 8100. Their address is PO Box 433, Moorgate Place, London EC2P 2BJ. Their website address is www.icaew.co.uk.

The Institute of Chartered Accountants in Scotland is on 0131 225 5673, and their address is 27 Queen Street, Edinburgh EH2 1LA. Their website address is www.icas.org.uk.

The Institute of Chartered Accountants in Ireland can be contacted on 00353 1668 0400 and at www.icai.ie.

There's also the Association of Chartered Certified Accountants (ACCA) on 020 7242 6855. They are based at 29 Lincoln's Inn Fields, London WC2A 3EE, and their website address is www.acca.org.uk.

PAYING TAX

The government's Tax Credit Helpline is on 0845 609 5000.

The self-assessment helpline facility is on 0845 9000 444. They will talk you through the basics of doing a tax return.

The Patent Office – in case you need help on copywriting your idea – has a helpline on 08459 500 505 and a website www.intellectual-property.gov.uk.

FIND A UNION

The Trades Union Congress, has a helpline for people wanting to find a union: call 0870 600 4882.

7 BUILDING A NEST

Even the most nomadic often yearn for a place to hang their hat, rest their slippered feet, soak up their favourite TV programmes and chill out to their treasured music with a few chocolate bars or a takeaway. Nothing beats having a place to call home.

Of course, the reality is a little less than romantic: renting or living with parents can often mean that the resting, TV and music bit turns into a row about what to watch, what to listen to and who gets Granddad's cosy old armchair.

That's when your thoughts might turn to having your own place. 'Wouldn't it be nice,' you say to yourself, 'just to come home and be able to do what I want when I want?'

And it's easier to buy your own place than ever before. Would you believe that until the 1970s women were not allowed to take out mortgages on their own? No wonder single females are now the fastest group of new property owners.

If you've got a regular job, you're not in too much debt and you've got to breaking point with having to share your PlayStation 2, then getting a mortgage is as easy as filling in a bit of paper.

It's the other things that can be a bit more difficult ...

WHEN IS THE RIGHT TIME TO BUY?

House prices go up and down like yo-yos. Predicting when is the time to snap up a bargain is impossible.

William, an insurance salesman, now retired, was one of the lucky ones. 'My house was worth a hundred and fifty thousand when we bought it in 1987. It went up to two hundred and fifty thousand in 1989 and then came crashing down to a hundred thousand not long after. Now, in 2002, it's worth nearly four hundred thousand.'

But for every William you've got a Maria and Nigel. 'We bought a house in St Albans for forty thousand,' says Maria. 'We borrowed forty thousand from the bank to buy it, a one-hundred-per-cent mortgage. Soon afterwards its value dropped to thirty-five thousand, then to thirty thousand. We wanted to move to Bristol because of work and we had to sell it for less than a mortgage, taking out a ten-thousand-pound loan to make up for the negative equity. If we had been able to hold on to it, it would have been worth about eighty thousand now.'

Then of course there is the emotional clock ticking away. Do you buy on your own, or wait till you are married/in a committed relationship?

'I gave up on the idea of buying a place with the right girl years ago,' says Andy. 'After a string of relationship break-ups I realised what I really needed was my own home. Now I'm working on the wife-and-marriage bit. But I have the security of knowing that at the end of each working day I can go back to my own place.'

'I kept my little flat in Manchester even when I got married,' says Helen. 'It wasn't very romantic but that little flat is my bolt hole. I've been known to stay there when we have a row. It's really great to have your own space.'

HOW IMPORTANT ARE HOUSE PRICES?

'House prices are always flitting around,' says Ruth, a financial adviser. 'I've seen them crash, soar, stabilise at least twenty times. It's a cycle that seems to keep repeating itself.'

The property boom that has engulfed the nation since the late 1990s has sent many would-be buyers into a panic. There is a bit of the now-or-never or oh-my-God-I'll-never-be-able-to-buy-a-place-if-I-don't-buy-now factor. The right time will depend on a few things, not just the state of the economy.

WHEN CAN I AFFORD IT?

Remember that you're already paying rent each month and probably have been for a few years. Sit down and tot up how much you've spent, because that's what finally persuaded Lynda, a 32-year-old with an aversion to financial commitment, to become a fully paid-up member of the property-owning set. She finally took the plunge after working out that in ten years she'd spent a whopping £30,000 on renting. 'That money's going towards lining some landlord's – well, several landlords' – pockets. I could have paid off half a house or a flat in that time.

'And it seemed a natural progression. Greed got the better of me and now that six hundred pounds [in rent] is going towards my future. I'd been waiting for a relationship to take off in the hope of moving in with a guy. But now I'm determined to do it on my own.'

If you have problems keeping up with your rent, you probably aren't ready. On the other hand, having the discipline of a mortgage may make you more financially astute. 'It was the usual story: landlord decides to sell up,' laments Linda. 'At the grand old age of thirty-five I decided I had to buy, despite having a lifestyle that requires lots of disposable income. Funnily enough, once I had my new pad I stayed in more, invited mates round. My expenses all went on the house, and I loved it.'

DEALING WITH YOUR DEBTS

Taking on a mortgage when you're up to your eyeballs in debt is tough, but it is possible. In fact it's not *having* debts: it's how you manage them that counts. If you are still paying off your store card each month, then you're actually a fairly safe bet for a bank. Whereas if you're still juggling Peter the credit card to pay off Paul the loan, then you may need to revise your attitude to your cash.

Sometimes, having a mortgage can end up being a good discipline. Sam, aged 38, found that taking on a mortgage meant she spent less on clothes. 'Well, it's about time I started buying bed sheets instead of stilettos! Although both come in very handy when you have your own place,' she says. 'I took on a mortgage when I was still studying, but I was married and we did have a young baby. It was tough getting the deposit together but I was a sponsored student doing an engineering PhD. I still had a student loan but because I could afford the repayments the bank gave me the mortgage.'

> ### *The renter's dilemma*
>
> **I'm thirty-six and I've been renting for fifteen years now. Is it time to bite the bullet and buy a place?**
>
> It depends why you haven't bought. Property ownership is a bigger deal in the UK than it is in, say, France. Maybe the idea of having a mortgage scares you sick. Fair enough: not everyone is cut out for owning their own home.

IF YOU CAN'T AFFORD IT

So you can't afford to go it alone. What are your options? Here are a few suggestions.

SISTER OR BROTHERLY LOVE

Kat decided to buy in London. Her job as a picture editor means she has to stay in the capital because she gets more work there. 'I decided to buy with my younger sister,' she says. 'That way we could afford a flat in a fairly OK part of town. And we have the security of knowing that there are two of us paying the mortgage.'

GO WITH A FRIEND

Paul bought with his childhood friend Simon. 'I wanted to get on the property ladder,' he says. 'My best mate wanted to buy a second home but didn't have quite enough cash to stretch to a second mortgage. Putting our incomes together meant we could afford a bigger place. We've made appropriate legal agreements because I own a slightly bigger share than he does. We've even got it down on paper that, if one of us comes into some cash and the other wants to move or gets married, the one still staying in the house gets first refusal on being able to buy out the other one.'

PAL UP WITH A PARTNER

This is a big emotional as well as financial step, so, if you are going to buy with your partner, then make sure you've got adequate legal provisions sorted out.

DECIDING WHERE TO LIVE

IS IT AFFORDABLE?

You know where you want to live, but whether you can set your roots down there will come down to that age old question of money. You want a two-bedroom flat but can you afford it? If you can't afford the area you live in, look at somewhere more affordable. Marianne, tired of looking at 'overpriced' two-bedroom flats in London, decided to rent in Brighton before buying a place there. 'London was too expensive, so I decided to get to know another part of the southeast. I found I loved it, and when I was looking for somewhere to live I knew what areas were dodgy and which ones weren't.'

When you are looking at affordability you'd be advised to carry out a mortgage check with your bank to find out how much you can actually borrow. 'I'd set my heart on a flat in Bath, but it wasn't till I checked out how much I could borrow that I realised there was no way I could borrow the amount I needed,' said Zoe.

Other things to take into consideration

£   **Council tax** – how much will you be paying? Areas, even within the same city, can charge very different levels of tax.

£   **Maintenance charges** – flats, freehold or not, will require you, as part of your deeds, to make regular repairs. This is also for the cost of maintaining shared and communal areas.

£   **Listed buildings** – some homes need to have other repairs made to them. 'I live by the seafront in Eastbourne,' says Mark, 'and, because it's a Grade II listed building, I have to make sure it's painted at least every five years.'

£   **Ground rent** – this is another extra you will have to pay if you're in leasehold flats. This is the money that the landlord charges you for having your building on his/her land. You are more likely to pay this kind of rent if you live in a flat in the city.

MAKE SURE YOU FEEL COMFORTABLE

There's no point in living somewhere simply because it is affordable, though. 'I couldn't buy in Manchester, so I travelled a little further away, somewhere I knew I could afford and commute from,' says Fiona. 'I also knew a couple of people living there already. Thing is that couple soon moved away – because they needed a bigger place. I was left stuck in a town where people were just as unfriendly as before. There's not a lot to do here, either. I've made a huge mistake and I want to get out.'

OTHER OPTIONS FOR CASH-STRAPPED HOUSE HUNTERS

A FORMER COUNCIL HOUSE OR FLAT

In London, where property is beyond the reach of the average wage-earner, buying a former local authority property can be one of the few ways of affording somewhere almost central. But these places do tend to be cheaper for a reason.

There are a few things you should be aware of if you're buying a former council flat.

£ **Beware of expenses. Have all the flats in the block been sold off? If they haven't, the council could still be making repairs to the block. Council tenants won't have to pay but you could be saddled with an unwanted bill for thousands of pounds.**

£ **Mind your neighbours. Sharing with neighbours who don't own their property could be an uncomfortable mix. Some of these people might feel resentment. 'I got graffiti saying "capitalist bastard" daubed on my door,' says Kay. 'In the end I rented it out.'**

£ **Check out the landlord. If the council still owns the freehold of the property, you could do worse. Councils as landlords tend to be more responsible, and they aren't going to do a runner with your money.**

DO-IT-YOURSELF HOME OWNERSHIP

These are offered by local housing associations but are options available only for families on low incomes. They allow you to get on the property ladder by paying part rent and part mortgage. As the years go by you can increase the mortgage element, so that you gradually own your own place.

If you are single you may be eligible but getting on a DIY scheme will depend on the availability of housing where you live. You need to contact your local authority for the housing associations that build in your borough.

It may also be difficult getting a mortgage, because a lot of banks are reluctant to lend money towards these schemes.

BUYING AT AN AUCTION

The houses you can buy at auction are normally either the subject of repossession or a property whose owner has died. You need to buy a catalogue or register with an auctioneer that specialises in selling homes. Check the property pages of your local paper for auctioneers in your area.

HOUSING CO-OPS

In London, where prices are sky-high, some would-be owners are clubbing together to form housing co-operatives. One good example of a housing co-op is a block of flats by the Oxo Tower on London's South Bank. Housing co-ops are a private version of housing associations and are set up as companies with a committee managing them. There's often a long waiting list, and you never completely own your house (the housing co-op keeps a share), although you do benefit from rises in house prices if you want to sell it on.

FINDING A PLACE

Most people looking to buy a home head straight to their local estate agent. It is a good starting point but estate agents are not the only way of finding your dream pad.

ESTATE AGENTS EXPLAINED

Estate agents act as go-betweens, liaising between the person selling the house or flat and the people wanting to buy it. They make their money by taking a commission from the seller. The commission is normally a percentage of the selling price, so it's in the estate agent's interest to sell the house to the highest bidder.

Estate agents have had quite a good run over the last few years, and you can find at least two or three estate agents' shops in an average-sized town. Even if you don't want to buy through an estate agent, they are good places to start your house hunting, because, by visiting a few in one area, you can get an idea of what is and isn't a reasonable price to pay for property.

Gazumping – it still happens When you make an offer on a place, and the home owner accepts it, they are still not legally obliged to sell you the property. Up until you exchange contracts (see below) the owner could still sell the property to someone offering more cash. This is known as *gazumping* and is illegal in Scotland, where sellers and buyers sign a legal contract as soon as an offer is made. So you could have paid out hundreds in legal fees only for an unscrupulous owner, or estate agent who is still letting other people view the pad you've offered to buy, to offer it to someone tendering more cash.

Gazumping has often been blamed on the fact that the whole house-buying process in England and Wales takes so long – from a few months to a year in some cases. There are moves afoot to bring in legal contracts in England and Wales, but this is still a long way off. In the meantime, some estate agents have introduced 'buyers' packs' to speed up house buying.

BUYING PRIVATELY

Local shops, newspapers (especially evening papers), *Loot* and the property sections of some of the national newspapers all have sections where private buyers advertise.

Pros of buying privately

- £   It may be cheaper, because the seller won't have to take into account the estate agent's commission.
- £   Buying on the Internet allows you to search vast swathes of areas for affordable homes.
- £   You don't have to worry about estate agents keeping the place on the market.

Cons of buying privately

- £   You can still get gazumped.
- £   You don't have the protection of an estate agent if things go wrong.
- £   It can take longer.

Helen has a tale to tell on that last point above. 'I found my place on the Internet,' she says. 'But I did miss the face-to-face contact, and I feel that because I wasn't able to ring up anyone and hassle them it took longer for things to get done.'

BUYING ON THE INTERNET

Estate agents often have accompanying websites, allowing you to widen your search for suitable homes and to check whether you can afford to live in the area you have set your heart on. Often, general independent websites will include homes sold both privately and through estate agents, allowing you an even bigger spread of the available housing in your area of choice.

WHEN YOU'VE FOUND A PLACE

MAKING AN OFFER

When you 'make an offer' on a property and it's accepted, you'll need to make sure that the home is taken off the market. This means that it is now 'subject to contract' and cannot be viewed by any more prospective buyers.

'I found my perfect pad in Clapham, southwest London,' says Samuel. 'It's a very popular area, and I didn't want to miss out, so I put in an offer right there and then. Thing is, I reckoned the estate agent was still letting people look at the flat, so I got my mum and my dad to ring the estate agent expressing an interest in the flat. On both occasions the estate agent offered to let them see the flat. I decided to withdraw my offer because I did not trust the estate agent.'

Be insistent with the estate agent because you're well within your rights to make sure that no one else is able to view the place.

DO YOU OFFER THE ASKING PRICE?

Not if you think it's too high. Marianne, see earlier, did her research. 'I'd seen this place on the market and the estate agent said it had been for sale for quite some time. I'd worked out for myself that it was overpriced. So I took a chance and offered ten thousand pounds less. They said they'd go eight thousand lower but throw in the oven and a sofa. A result.'

SORTING OUT THE BASICS

If you haven't got one, you'll need to get yourself a solicitor. You can ask friends, colleagues or your parents if they know a good conveyancer. These are solicitors who specialise in property law and will do all the legal checks and property searches for you.

Check with the solicitor how much they charge. It can be anything from £500 to more than £1,000. It's then up to the solicitor to make sure that the place you're buying doesn't have any hidden surprises. Helen found that a motorway was going to be built down the road from her dream flat. 'That's what you pay a solicitor for. I still decided to buy, but at least I had all the facts. A solicitor will also look at things you might not even consider.'

But it didn't quite end there. 'The flat had a gorgeous roof garden but because it was a leasehold flat there were conditions attached. Pretty big conditions, in fact. I found out that I couldn't actually use it. In the end I had to pay out five hundred pounds to change the lease, but can you just imagine what would've happened if we hadn't found out?'

Tax warning! Aside from solicitor's fees, you'll have to pay the government a tax called *stamp duty*, which is worked out as a percentage of the value of the home you are buying, if your home is under £60,000 you don't have to pay stamp duty. There are three levels of stamp duty: 1, 3 and 4 per cent. So, if you are buying a home worth between £60,001 and £250,000, you'll pay 1 per cent. For example, if you buy a home worth £70,000, you'll have to pay an upfront lump of £700. If your home is valued at between £250,001 and £500,000, the stamp duty goes up to 3 per cent – so, if you are buying a home worth £300,000, stamp duty will be £9,000. And, if it is worth £500,001 and over, you'll pay 4 per cent of its value in tax.

The chancellor is looking at raising the stamp duty limits because of the rise in house prices.

BUYING YOUR HOME

You've armed yourself with enough experts to shake an estate agent's sign at. Now you're going to need to sort out how you actually pay for it.

MORTGAGES: THE BASICS

If you haven't got the cash to pay for your home, then you'll need to start looking into taking out a mortgage. Mortgages come in lots of different forms, but all of them are secured loans, unlike the personal loans in **Spending It**. A secured loan means that, if you don't keep up your repayments, the company that has lent you the cash can repossess your home.

The best thing you can do when you buy a house is to have a good deposit so that you don't have to borrow the whole amount. If you have to borrow more than 90 per cent of what your would-be home is worth you'll also have to pay a high lending fee, a mortgage indemnity premium. This is an insurance the mortgage company takes out and you have to pay for.

If you can, try to put down a deposit that equals around ten per cent of the price you have offered to buy. You can get away with five per cent but the more of a deposit you put down the more mortgages you can choose from, and the cheaper the interest rate you'll pay.

For example, if you're buying a £70,000 place you'll need to have around £3,500 plus the stamp duty and the solicitor's fees. This can work out at about £5,500 in total. But remember that, if you do have a deposit, your loan will be cheaper. Helen, for example, managed to cobble together some cash by borrowing three thousand pounds from her uncle.

Mortgages may also include extras, such as cashback, a free survey and even free insurance. Below are some frequently asked questions, followed by some information about the various types of mortgage you can get.

What can I borrow? If you're buying and you are the only one earning, your bank or building society will let you borrow up to three and a half times your annual salary. So, if you are earning

£25,000, you can borrow around £87,000 – give or take the odd thousand.

Some banks will lend you more than that, but you have to ask yourself whether you really can afford it. If you are part of a couple and you are both earning, then the bank will let you borrow two and a half times your *joint* income: if you are both on £25,000, then your joint income is £50,000, so you can borrow £125,000.

I can't get a mortgage – something about a dodgy credit record?
As with loans and credit cards, mortgage companies check your credit record first to see if you are a good bet. If you haven't been bad with money in the past it may be something else on your credit record that's stopping your bank from lending you money. The only way to be sure is to get a copy of your credit record (see **Debt: The Good the Bad and the Ugly** for details on how to do this).

Can more than two buy a place together? Victoria went into a form of partnership with her parents, and they all own a third each. 'The way they see it, it's their pension. I will eventually buy them out when I can afford it. But to live in London and to get on the property ladder I needed their help.'

So if I'm self-employed I'll never get a mortgage? You may still be able to get a mortgage. If you've been self-employed for three years or more lenders will ask you for three years' worth of accounts. This will give them an idea of how much you earn and how much you can afford. There are several specialised lenders who do arrange mortgages for self-employed people, but your choice may be more limited.

'I managed to get a mortgage even though I'd only been working as a freelance for a year,' says Sam. 'The stipulation was that I put down a twenty-five-per-cent deposit, which wasn't too hard because I'd been made redundant and had a lot of cash in the bank.'

MORTGAGES: PICK AND MIX, BUT MORE EXPENSIVE

It can be difficult to decide what kind to have. You can get a mortgage from your bank but it's probably best to shop around. You used to be able to get mortgages only from building societies, but now everyone's in on the game. If you really want to do your research, get proper financial advice from an independent financial adviser, who is able to sell the mortgages of most companies.

If you've got a good relationship with your bank, try them, or go on the Internet. 'I used a Web search engine. I found so many mortgage finders that it was really easy to spot a deal,' said Helen.

Do your homework There's nothing like reading up to help you work out a good mortgage deal. The Saturday and Sunday personal-finance pages of all the national newspapers publish best-buy deals. (They're great for checking up on savings – see **Saving** – as well as mortgage rates while you're at it.) There are plenty of financial websites and the Financial Services Authority has got in on the act with some online comparison tables where you can compare different interest rates.

Let's take some more questions.

How do I know what a good mortgage is? Like loans and credit cards, mortgages also have APRs. The APR will include how much interest you pay (see below), plus when it must be paid; a fee you pay to the lender, like insurance; and when these fees are charged. It does not include penalties for missed payments or penalties if you pay the mortgage off early.

What kinds of mortgages are there? All mortgage products – as advisers call them – are based on interest rates. This is the major part of the mortgage and all mortgage interest rates are based on the Bank of England's base rate – but it's how they use the interest rate that makes the mortgage different.

What about repayment versus interest-only mortgages? With a repayment mortgage, you slowly repay the actual cost of your home as well as the interest.

When you take out an interest-only mortgage you also take out an investment policy to cover the main part of your home. This is because you are paying only the interest, not the whole loan. The loan part is paid off with the investment section at the end of your mortgage period.

Are interest-only mortgages any good? The problem with interest-only mortgages is that the products that you take out to cover the investment part, endowments, have been doing badly in recent years. Once, people took out interest-only mortgages and then an endowment and the endowment would make a lot of money and give cash to spare on top of paying off the mortgage.

Endowments are not covered here, but if you have one you would be best contacting the Financial Services Authority for more advice. You can take out an ISA mortgage, which works like an interest-only mortgage, but you put your money into an ISA instead.

MORTGAGES: ALL KINDS OF EVERYTHING ...

These are the different kinds of mortgage around.

£ **Fixed rate** – this kind of mortgage gives you the same interest rate for a period, between three and five years in most cases. This means that your mortgage payments are the same every month for that fixed period. After then your mortgage becomes a standard variable-rate mortgage (see below).

£ **Capped rate** – this rate does change but will be capped at a certain level for a fixed time, and will not go an agreed amount above the Bank of England's base rate.

£ **Base tracker rate** – this tracks the Bank of England's base rate and is guaranteed to be a set amount above it.

£ **Variable** – this rate follows the Bank of England's base rate. It can go up and down. In fact, it was people with variable interest rates who were most affected by the dramatic rise in the bank rate in the early 1990s.

£ **Discounted rate** – this is like the capped rate, but is fixed below the base rate for a special period, normally between three and five years.

£ **One hundred per cent** – these are normally discounted, capped, tracker or variable mortgages. The difference is that you are not expected to put down a deposit.

£ **Flexible** – these may have a fixed interest rate but, instead of having to pay off a set amount each month, you have only a minimum repayment to make. This can allow you in effect to overpay or pay off your mortgage early. You may even be able to take payment holidays. The interest rates on flexible mortgages are normally fixed.

£ **CAT mortgages** – these are standards, like the ISA. CAT stands for *charges, access and terms*. A CAT mortgage isn't endorsed by the government but it does have to abide by particular terms. These include things such as interest rates: if they fall, your mortgage will have to drop its interest rate in a calendar month. A CAT mortgage cannot charge more than a £150 booking fee.

£ **Pension mortgages** – when you take your pension you can use the lump sum from your pension to pay off your mortgage (see Building a Nest for more on pensions and lump sums). These are somewhat like the interest-only mortgages above. The problem with these is that the earliest you can pay off your mortgage is when you start getting your pension, so you may have to wait until you are at least fifty.

A very important issue to note: With all these mortgages you may be charged if, for whatever happy reason, you are able to pay back your home loan before the usual 25 years are up. The penalty you are charged will depend on how long you have had the mortgage for: the longer you've had it, the less the penalty. So, if you pay off a mortgage just three years after taking it out, expect to pay back a lot.

MORTGAGES: WHAT YOU PAY

What happens with interest rates on all these mortgages?
Mortgage interest rates are based on the Bank of England's base rate, which is set once a month. But how much you really pay depends on the *annual percentage rate* (APR) imposed when you take out your mortgage. As a guide, mortgage at 5 per cent interest means you pay 5 per cent of the total you borrowed each year in interest.

Helen's £60,000 mortgage attracts £3,600 each year in interest. 'I pay this monthly, so it gets split into twelve bits, so I pay three hundred pounds a month,' she says.

What about the loan part? As Helen points out, 'That's the interest part of my mortgage – I still have to pay the loan back, so I still owe sixty thousand. Divided up over twenty-five years, that works out at two hundred pounds a month. So, if I add the three hundred for the interest and the two hundred for the loan, I end up paying five hundred [a month].'

So what type should I go for?

A security blanket for first-timers: fixed rate Helen was a first-time buyer so she went for a fixed-rate mortgage. 'With that I paid the same amount each month for five years,' she explains. 'It was good to know that I was paying five hundred pounds and that was it, even when interest rates went up. When you first set up home you need to know where your money is going. I liked knowing that I could afford to buy furniture and go out. The only bugger is when interest rates go down and your mortgage doesn't. You are tied in, so if you do want to swap your mortgage your lender will normally make you pay an indemnity fee.'

Seasoned shopper gets bargain Jay, who bought with her husband Tom, got a shock when her fixed rate came to an end. 'Our mortgage went up by a hundred pounds a month,' she says. 'So what we did was remortgage on another fixed-rate deal with another bank. We looked around on the Internet as well as speaking to our bank and a financial adviser.'

If you can hack it – a variable rate If you reckon interest rates are going to get lower, then a variable-rate mortgage could be suitable. You have got to bear in mind that variable rates go up as well as down.

'When we took out the mortgage for our flat in St Albans it was a variable,' says Simon. 'Interest rates went up to twelve per cent and we ended up forking out, at one point, about eight hundred pounds on a mortgage that was normally less than half that.'

Tracker, capped and discounted rates – taking a calculated risk This one is like the variable-rate plan, but you do have some protection against rates going sky-high. 'I took my capped rate out at a time when property prices were low but the interest rate was high – well, eight per cent,' says Mandy. 'Now they have dropped I'm laughing because my payments have gone from seven hundred pounds a month to three hundred.'

No deposit doesn't mean no home Helen had to go for a 100 per cent mortgage. 'I had no deposit but couldn't be done with renting any more, so I looked around. The only problem with a hundred-percenter is that you do pay a higher rate of interest and you have to pay mortgage indemnity. There's less choice so I'm on a capped mortgage that still goes up and down, but it guarantees not to go above a certain level. You can still get stung if rates go up. But I've got a lodger in my flat who helps me pay the mortgage.'

MORTGAGES: PAYING THEM OFF

Nearly all mortgages, with a few exceptions, are for 25 years. So when you take out a mortgage you are promising to pay it back within that time. But because most of us move several times, and take out further mortgages in order to get ourselves bigger places, you might end up spending forty years paying off a mortgage.

'My parents ended up paying a mortgage for nearly forty-five years,' says Helen. 'The first home they bought was only worth two thousand pounds. But as they moved up the property ladder they ended up borrowing more. They needed a bigger home to accommodate all of us kids. I expect I will be in the same situation.'

There are mortgages that offer you the option of paying the whole thing back in ten years; they work out expensive in the short term but, because you end up paying less interest, they may save you thousands.

There has been clamour, what with rising house prices, for mortgages that allow house buyers to spread their mortgage paying over thirty years or more. Keep an eye out for developments on this; it could change the whole mortgage market.

MORTGAGES: WHERE TO BUY

You can go through a mortgage broker or adviser who will either be 'tied', which means they sell only the mortgages of certain companies, or they can be independent, when they are able to sell nearly all mortgages. Brokers will charge commission, in which case the mortgage company gives them an agreed percentage or introductory fee, or they can charge you a one-off fee and waive their commission.

Going through your bank You can get a mortgage through your bank, but they will be able to offer you only their own mortgages, which means you will not be able to compare different rates.

You can now get mortgages through supermarkets or on the Internet. Internet mortgages are cheaper because they often come fee-free. Remember that the more searching that has to be done to find you a mortgage, such as with a broker or adviser, the larger the fee you will pay.

'I found out about one really good adviser on the Internet,' says Helen. 'It searches for the best mortgage to suit your circumstances with an online calculator. This asks what sort of home you are buying, how much deposit you are putting down. It came up with about twenty suitable matches with the estimated monthly payment. I was able to have a good look around, including changing my deposit amount to see how much my mortgage would be if I put more or less down at the beginning.'

Helen forgot to mention that she also pays other things as well as the APR. This includes the fee she paid when she took out the mortgage – this differs for each mortgage firm – and any penalties she may have to pay if she misses a payment.

Is it still worth it? The value of property usually goes up. So, while you may end up paying £120,000 over 25 years, the chances are that your £60,000 home may end up being worth about £200,000. Marianne's London flat has doubled in value since she bought it ten years ago. 'Now I can afford to buy another flat and rent my first one out,' she says. 'It's not like I'm rich. I've just spent wisely.'

Who sets the interest rate? The Bank of England has a committee, the Monetary Policy Committee, that meets each month to decide whether interest rates should go higher or lower, or remain the same. 'Keeping an eye on the financial papers is a sure way to tell what way things are going,' says Sara. 'Just by keeping an eye on things you can prepare yourself for a hit on your mortgage payments.'

If you can't afford to pay If at some point during the repayment of your mortgage you suddenly can't afford to pay, speak to your mortgage company. They may be able to help you by reducing your mortgage payments or allowing you to suspend them until you are back on your feet. Or you can contact some of the debt helplines in **Debt: The Good the Bad and the Ugly**.

BUYING THE PROPERTY

Your money is sorted. Now there are some other things you'll need to do.

The survey When you buy a house the bank will do a credit check to make sure you are creditworthy. Then, as banks do, it will make sure that the house you're buying is worth what the person selling it says it is. The bank in effect owns the house – but not for ever. To do this the bank will charge you £200 or more to carry out a survey. Surveyors will make sure that the house you are buying is not about to fall down. They will look at things such as damp, subsidence and whether it needs a new roof.

Helena found that two dodgy surveys helped her work out what kind of home not to buy. 'I soon sussed out that flat-roofed homes were going to require big-time maintenance,' she says. 'I spent six hundred pounds on two surveys but at least I knew the place I did buy was a sure bet.'

What if the survey shows problems? Sometimes the bank will still lend you the money if there are only a few things wrong, such as a patch of damp or some loose roof tiles. But, if a survey comes back with a lot of problems, you may be best to start looking for another property – even though you've paid your money, you'll end up saving in the long run.

Three kinds of survey You normally have to pay about £200 for a survey, but if you want a more detailed one you can get a Homebuyers Survey. These cost a bit more. Some people go for a full structural survey, which is as complicated as it sounds and can cost £1,000 or more.

These more detailed surveys are useful if you want to extend or renovate your home. When Jane and Tony bought their place they had a full structural survey. 'We wanted to build an extension out the back and needed to know what the state of the garden was,' says Jane.

What if the sale falls through? Having been gazumped, Jacqui was nearly put off buying a place altogether. 'The government is doing stuff to try to speed up the whole process of buying a house but it's still one of the risks you take. I'd advise anyone to try to make contact – if they can – with the person selling the house you want to buy. Estate agents can act as a barrier, but nothing beats that personal contact; and, if they know you, the seller may be less likely to offer the house to someone else offering more money. Not everyone is motivated by money!'

How long does it take? Home buying is a slow process, although the government is trying to speed it up (see above). It can take months, especially if there is a 'chain'. This refers to the situation many buyers find themselves in when the person they are buying from is waiting for the next person to buy, and so on. You'll know you're ready to move when you exchange contracts. You then wait a few days for completion, when you get the keys to your place. 'What a feeling of relief it was!' says Helen. 'It was worth it.'

WHEN NESTING EQUALS RENTING

BUYING TO LET

Some people get so frustrated with being unable to get on the first rung of the property ladder that they decide to go for the buying-to-let option. This means you are buying a property, not a home, solely for investment. The bank is lending you the cash on the basis that you are going to be letting it out to other people.

Making yourself a landlord is not easy: you'll have to make sure that the place you are buying is in an area, ideally a city, where people will earn good money to rent a place; and you have to make sure that the rent you are charging is more than the mortgage you are paying – this is to make sure that you are covering any additional expenses such as work on the building or household appliances. Remember that money you receive in rent also counts as income and is subject to tax via self-assessment (see the end of **Your Working Life** for details of accountants).

Hazel went back home for her buy-to-let place. 'I wanted to buy in London but it got way too expensive,' she says. 'I turned thirty and wanted to feel that the cash I had saved up would be going somewhere. In the end I decided to buy a three-bedroom place near Dublin, where my parents come from, and rent it out while I stayed renting in London. I got a special buy-to-let mortgage, which took account of any gaps I may have in renting the place.'

RENTING OUT A ROOM

This is an option if you are struggling with your mortgage. Renting out a room means looking at the legal implications again. You have to go to a solicitor and get a short-term letting agreement with whomever you are going to rent the room to, and you will also have to pay tax on any rental income you make.

LEASEHOLD VERSUS FREEHOLD

When you buy somewhere you may see the words 'lease' followed by a number of years: for example, 'lease is for 88 years' or 'lease runs for another 70 years'. What this means is that someone, a landlord, owns the land on which the home you are buying is built. That person is known as the *freeholder*. When you buy a freehold house you are the owner of the property for life.

If you are a *leaseholder* you'll still own the place but you may have to pay certain fees to the landlord: maintenance charges for looking after communal areas, for instance, and a ground rent for 'renting' out the land your home is built on. The idea of leaseholding is a bit of a throwback to when large landowners charged people to build on their land. In any case, your solicitor will be able to tell you how much you have to pay and when.

Leases may also have conditions attached: you may, for example, have to have the outside painted every two years; or you may not be allowed to have pets (that's a bit extreme but it can happen). Leasehold properties nearly always tend to be flats.

LEASEHOLDERS GET NEW RIGHTS

Most leaseholders have the right to extend the lease for ninety years after they have lived there for two years or more. It is less complicated and costs less than buying a share of the freehold.

In July 2002 the law changed so that it became easier for leaseholders to extend their leases. At the same time the government created a new form of ownership for flat owners called *commonhold*. You can become a commonholder by teaming up with other people in your block of flats and agreeing to form a commonhold, which works like a company. If you are interested in doing this give the Leasehold Advisory Service a call (the number is in the **Resources** section).

If you are a commonholder, you do not have to answer to a landlord, and all the people living in the same block of flats have the same rights. Also, you don't have to worry about renewing your lease. Commonholders in the same property have to set up associations that are registered with the Land Registry, and they have to get together to vote on important issues, such as maintenance charges.

While not a freeholder as such, a commonholder should not have to worry about landlords charging rip-off ground rents. If you want to know more about the other new commonholder rights you can check the finer details with the Leasehold Advisory Service.

HOW DO I KNOW MY PLACE IS LEASEHOLD?

Before you put in an offer for your home, check whether it is leasehold or freehold. If it is leasehold the estate agent, or whoever is selling the place, will be able to tell you how many years the lease has left. The longer the better, as mortgage companies do not like lending money to buy homes with only a few years left on the lease.

Once you buy your home, it's yours for good – if it's a freehold, that is. This means that you are the legal owner of the land and have to be responsible for the whole lot!

BUYING ABROAD

People are going further afield to get a slice of the property market, as with Hazel, above, who bought a property near Dublin. If you are interested in this it's a good idea to contact a solicitor who is familiar with the property law in the country where you are thinking of buying.

REMORTGAGING

Remortgaging is a fancy term for switching your mortgage. You can remortgage to save yourself cash, so, if interest rates drop and you are coming up to the end of your tie-in period, you can either look elsewhere or try to get a different mortgage with the same company as the old one.

You can also remortgage to raise extra cash to improve your existing home. 'We bought just before the real boom in London,' says Nick. 'It had been a real struggle because our last place got us into negative equity [see below]. We owed a few debts but we were able to make the mortgage repayments on the new house. Then, five years later, we had it valued and the house is worth nearly double.

'So we used the value of the house to go to the bank and remortgage on the new value. This gave us cash to pay off our debts and to start a new business – doing property development.

'Of course, you are still gambling on there not being a property-market crash. I think a lot of people have remortgaged their homes during the boom. It also means your payments will go up. For us it was a cheaper way of getting a loan.'

To remortgage you need to get your home valued by a surveyor. You can do this through the bank you want your mortgage with, or you can pay for one privately – find a local surveyor by getting in touch with the Royal Institute of Chartered Surveyors (see **Resources**). As long as your home is in good condition, you should be able to remortgage for its existing value with no problems.

YOU'VE GOT ASSETS

You can also use your home as collateral. This means you can use it to secure loans that you might not otherwise get. Of course, your home could be repossessed if you fail to make any repayments.

WHAT'S NEGATIVE EQUITY?

A scary phrase for homeowners. Many have already found themselves in this position. It means that your home is worth less than the mortgage you've got on it. When you are in a negative-equity situation you end up paying a monthly mortgage that does not represent the value of the house.

Of course, if you can still pay the mortgage you can hang on until prices rise, because if the past is anything to go by they still do.

But the chances are that, if your house has dropped, others have, too, and that suggests the economy is not very buoyant. This could mean that interest rates have been increased, which, in turn, could mean that you end up paying more on your mortgage. If you can't afford this you may be forced to sell your home for a loss.

These mutually exclusive circumstances occurred during the big recession of the early 1990s.

Will house prices always keep falling and then rising? House buying is such a large part of the economic psyche of the UK. It fuels so many things, such as spending, borrowing and manufacturing. Low interest rates – which make mortgages cheaper and therefore make more people want to buy, and therefore increase house prices – are not always guaranteed. Interest rates depend on lots of things, and the world economy has become so interdependent that a recession in Japan, for example, soon leads to a full-blown global economic shutdown.

A good example is the stock market and share prices. They're incredibly unpredictable but a share bought twenty years ago has normally increased its value. Property is not a short-term investment any more.

'I've got friends who bought properties specifically for the reason that they'd sell them on, and some of them got stung when prices dropped,' says Helen. 'Buying a house is about buying yourself a home. Somewhere that's yours and isn't dependent on the whims of your landlord.'

IF YOU ARE RENTING

Not everyone seeks to buy a home. Many people choose to rent, or feel that renting is economically the better option. As with buying, though, there are questions, questions, questions. Here are some answers.

How much rent should I be paying? Try to pay less than a third of your monthly salary. This will allow you enough cash to save and pay off any debts as well as allow you a decent standard of living.

Which laws concern renting? The Housing Act of 1996 made changes to the way houses and flats are rented. These renting agreements allow landlords to charge a full market rent. They also make it easier for landlords to evict people if they cause a nuisance to neighbours or they don't pay rent. There are three types of arrangement if you are renting: an *assured tenancy*, an *assured shorthold tenancy* and a *licence to occupy*.

The first two will apply if you moved in after 15 January 1989, are renting privately and the house is you main home. A licence to occupy is the kind of agreement you would go into if your landlord was living with you.

What can I expect of my landlord? The money you pay should ensure that you live in accommodation that's fit for human habitation.

You will normally be asked by your landlord for a deposit, which is one month's rent in advance, especially if you have a short-term tenancy agreement with your landlord. This agreement, which will take the form of a signed contract, means that your landlord has to give you two month's notice if he or she wants to evict you. It also means that you are obliged to give them a month's notice if you want to move out – this length of time can change, so make sure you check your rental agreement.

'My landlord used to live with us,' says Rebecca. 'When she decided to move she took the fridge and the phone, and it was only when I kicked up a real fuss and threatened to leave that she agreed to leave them behind.'

Landlords don't have to leave you essentials such as phones, vacuum cleaners and so forth unless it is specified in an inventory that you should have seen and signed when you moved in. If you've got a fridge that breaks down you should be able to ask your landlord to replace it. Things like washing machines tend still to be seen as luxuries, especially by stingy landlords.

What if my place is handled by a letting agency? A letting agency has been paid by the landlord to look after the renting of the property. In fact, if you've rented through a letting agency, it means the landlord is pretty serious about making sure things are above board. Property that has been let through an agency might be of a better standard than that rented privately, but bear in mind that the landlord might be charging extra in order to get back some of the cash they are having to pay the agency.

How much notice does a landlord have to give me if they want me to leave? If you have an assured shorthold tenancy, you need to be given two months' notice. If you have an assured tenancy you can remain in the property unless the landlord can prove they have grounds for possession, so the landlord does not have a right to repossess the property when your contract to rent ends.

Most rental agreements are shorthold tenancies.

What happens when my landlord won't pay back my deposit and I've done nothing wrong? You can go through the small-claims court to get your money back. This is why it's always important, even when renting through a letting agency, to make sure you have the landlord's contact details.

SOME EXTRA HELP

The Financial Services Authority does not regulate the selling of mortgages but it does have a lot of information, including tables, where you can compare the long-term cost of different mortgages. You can get leaflets by ringing the helpline on 0845 606 1234 or you can go online at www.fsa.gov.uk/consumer/.

Most UK mortgage lenders are members of the Council of Mortgage Lenders (CML). This means they have signed up to a voluntary code of conduct that promises to deal with customers fairly and squarely. You can check whether your mortgage company has signed up to the code online at www.cml.org.uk, or call the CML's helpline 020 7440 2255. There is also the Mortgage Code Arbitration Service on 020 7421 7444 or online at www.arbitrators.org.

Leaseholders Find out about your rights and the latest news on leaseholding on the Shelter housing website

www.shelternet.org.uk. Or check out the Leasehold Advisory
Service at www.lease-advice.org.uk or phone them on 020 7490
9580.

The real experts One really helpful place to go (not to say the
others mentioned are not!) is the Royal Institute of Chartered
Surveyors. The RICS is mainly responsible for training and
regulating surveyors (the guys who check out your house – see the
earlier information about surveys) but it also has a website that has
up-to-the-minute information on house-buying and house prices.
You could do worse than taking a really good look at
www.rics.org.uk or their address is 12 Great George Street, London
SW1P 3AD or you could phone them on 020 7222 7000.

8 GETTING OLD

Hands up who wants to get older. Hmm, thought not. The likes of Joan Collins, Tom Jones, Diana Rigg and Sean Connery may make turning older look glamorous, but the reality is that the things associated with getting older – wrinkles, grey hair, false teeth – are anything but.

Even more frightening for most people is the idea that they actually have to start putting money away to pay for their lifestyle in later years. Even worse, though, is that they're constantly being told that they can't put just a few pounds away each month: it has to be hundreds. And also that the money they do put away may not even be worth much!

It's enough to put you off pensions entirely. Well, maybe.

In other countries the whole idea of pensions isn't seen as boring at all. In fact in the United States they've taken the whole idea of pensions to a new level. 'I visited bars in New York and it seemed that in every bar/restaurant/coffee shop I went in to the waiters would be discussing their investment choices,' says Steven. 'I thought that these waiters were obviously paid well. It was only when I came back to the UK that someone told me most Americans have these pension plans. They don't look on them as pension plans: they look at them as shares. So they are really into them.'

But, if pensions still scare you, and they probably will at the moment, then you might like to look at other ways of saving for your retirement.

WHY SAVE FOR OLD AGE?

You either accept that you're going to have to work till you drop – and some people do – or you decide that at some stage in your life you want to be spending several months a year sunning yourself on faraway beaches without having to worry about how you're going to settle your credit-card bill.

As long a way off as it seems, the chances are that in older age you'll be more active than your grandparents were or even your parents are. Today's lifestyles give you greater expectations than those of your parents: more travel, more exotic food and more time spent indulging oneself.

Pension sceptic, Jacqui, says, 'I suppose it would be quite nice not to have to work for ever and not have to worry about always having to pay the mortgage, or worry how we'll afford our next holiday. Maybe it is something worth saving up for.'

The most obvious way of making sure you're not an old bag lady, or an old bag man, when you get older is to start stashing your cash away into a pension. It's probably one of the biggest financial commitments in terms of time, because you could be paying into it for thirty, maybe forty, years.

HOW PENSIONS WORK

A pension works like a savings account, except that you can't take any of the cash until you swap your suit for a pipe and slippers or Gucci heels for fluffy lounge mules. When you take on a pension plan, the accepted term is '*buying* a pension', but, whatever you call it, you are committing yourself to not seeing that money for some time.

Some pensions will let you take payment breaks, if, say, you have a baby or need to take time off work; but on the whole you'll be paying your pension money monthly or annually.

Because you don't pay tax on the cash you put into the pension, there are strict limits on how much you can put in, and this depends on how much you earn. This is to stop pensions being used by extremely wealthy people as ways of evading tax.

There are a lot of different kinds of pension. Different types are paid in different ways, but, if you are thinking of taking one out, there are some you need to know about.

£   Government pension – this is also known colloquially as the *old-age pension*, and is paid to everyone over the state retirement age if they've paid into the state earnings-related pension scheme, which is looked at below

£   Company pensions – these are set up for you by your firm; sometimes they'll even pay money in to match your own contributions
£   Private pensions – these are ones you set and pay into yourself
£   Stakeholder pensions – these are a government scheme that acts like a personal pension

---

Pension politics How much government pension you received used to depend entirely on how much you had paid in National Insurance contributions. But this was thought to be unfair to people who have had to give up work to look after children, or care for older or disabled relatives. So in 2001 and 2002 the government decided to help top up those people's pensions via a second pension scheme called the state second pension.

Let's look in more detail at those three types of pension.

GOVERNMENT PENSIONS

You can't begin receiving your government pension until you're 65. (With a private or company pension you can sometimes retire earlier, often as young as 50.)

The government's pension scheme has been around since World War Two. It was one of the great developments of the welfare state. Even so, state pensions don't pay that much. In April 2002, single pensioners received £75.50 a week while couples received £120.70 a week. At the moment the pension is the main way people who've retired can afford to live.

Two types of government pension Even government pensions have their complexities, so a little explanation is needed.

There's a *basic pension* for people who've paid National Insurance contributions while at work. Then there's an *additional state pension*, which in 2001 became dubbed the *state second pension*.

At the moment the government works out how much pension people get according to how much they paid in National Insurance contributions while they were working – this is called the *state earnings-related pension scheme*, or SERPS. People who are not working because they have to care for young children or, say, someone with a disability or long-term illness or an elderly relative will not get SERPS. Instead the government helps them out by putting cash into their state second pension.

Can I rely on the government pensions scheme? A tough question to answer. The reason the government gives lots of benefits to people paying into a private or company pension is that they are aware that, by the time you retire, the current state pension system may not be able to afford to pay you.

So how am I already paying into the state scheme? If you do not have a company pension you are probably already paying into the government scheme (SERPS). In paying National Insurance contributions – the bit of your salary that disappears but isn't given to the taxman – you are putting your money, or part of it, into a giant pensions pot (see **Your Working Life** for more on National Insurance contributions). But, because more and more of us are getting older, most of the money we pay into National Insurance is being paid out to help old people now. Quite simply, the government is running out of cash to pay pensions! There's a lot of debate as to whether there will be a pension scheme in twenty or thirty years' time simply because the government won't have enough money in the pension pot.

Should I stay in SERPS? It really depends on how much faith you have in the ability of the government's pension scheme. If you are paying a lot into your pension you might be able to afford to keep paying into SERPS. If you don't pay into SERPS, there is no government pension when you retire, and you'll have to rely on your private or company pension.

Isn't it compulsory to put money into a pension? No, it isn't. In some countries, such as Australia, the government makes people pay and, in 1997, there was pressure on the government to introduce the same kind of thing here. A Member of Parliament and former minister of social security, Frank Field, suggested a radical change to the pensions system but his ideas were believed to be too expensive. Making people pay into a pension is also a big moral dilemma for the government because it needs us to keep paying National Insurance to fund people who are retired now. So, if people start contributing to their own schemes, the government will find it hard to justify to us why we are paying National Insurance at all. Setting up a compulsory scheme might also be expensive – see below.

My boss has been told to start a pension scheme for us – isn't that compulsory? Yes – if there are more than five people in the firm. The government, as we've seen, wants to make as many people as possible save up for their retirement. Setting up a pension is not cheap, so what it did was encourage pension companies to set up low-cost plans called *stakeholder pensions* (see below).

COMPANY PENSIONS

If you're employed by a firm, you can join the company pension scheme. Usually, your company will also pay in a bit for you. It's not the same as the stakeholder scheme, because it's not normally low-cost.

Why a work pension? If your employer runs a pension scheme, it's usually a good idea to join. Your employer will be putting money into the pension for you and you get other benefits. You also get a tax-free lump sum when you retire from work and you can even take early retirement, whereas with the government scheme you have to be 65. You also get a pension if you become sick and have to give up work and your family may continue to get a pension if you die, albeit a reduced amount. There may be life insurance for your family, too.

The basics Your firm may be offering two kinds of pension: one that both you and your firm pay into, called a *contributory scheme*; and a *noncontributory scheme*, where your boss pays in but you don't have to. These kinds of pension are normally available to senior executives or people working for public services, such as teachers and nurses.

Once you've sorted out how you pay your money in you need to know what kind of pension your company is running.

Final-salary schemes Final-salary schemes are a dying breed, because – as you can imagine – they aren't cheap. If you are in a final-salary scheme you'll know about it. These are the *crème de la crème* of pension schemes. When you have a final-salary scheme you will get a pension that equals a certain proportion of your final salary when you retire.

Mike, who's 36, has watched his dad get a great pension. 'When my dad retired he was on a salary of forty thousand pounds,' he says. 'His pension was over twenty-six thousand, because he was paid two-thirds of his final salary. That's a very good pension but he's told me I can't expect to retire on anything near that: not only do I not get paid much, but I haven't even got a pension.'

Final-salary schemes are almost extinct: in 1991 nearly 6 million people working for private companies (those owned by shareholders or managers) were in a final-salary scheme; in 2000 this had dropped to about three million.

Money-purchase schemes This is a straightforward idea: you pay in regular amounts and whatever your money makes while it's invested in the scheme you get back as your pension. Your money purchases your pension – simple. Money-purchase plans are now the most popular kind of work pension plan.

STAKEHOLDER PENSIONS

The clamour for a private pension scheme to run alongside National Insurance contributions became so great in the late 1990s that the government felt it had to do something to allow everyone, not just employees of large firms, the chance to save their own pension. The stakeholder scheme is a cheaper version of a private pension because it doesn't have the same charges as most private pensions. It is now illegal for small firms with more than five employees not to have a stakeholder pension.

What makes stakeholder pensions different? Stakeholder schemes are really a hybrid kind of pension because they are more expensive than the government's pension but cheaper than a personal pension.

£   Cheaper charges: You pay only 1 per cent of the value of your pension fund each year. So, if your pension fund is worth £3,000 after a year (that's your payments plus whatever the fund has made), you'll pay the

£   pension company £30 to manage your money. Some personal pensions charge 5 per cent or more.

£   Cheap payments: You don't have to put in a great amount: £25 a month is enough.

£   Chopping and changing: You can choose when you put money in, and you are not penalised for taking breaks.

£   Free transfers: If you want to swap your pension money you don't have to pay for the privilege.

£   Lots of information: You get statements showing how much you have paid into your pension and regular forecasts of how much it will be worth when you give up work.

How do I know if I need one? At the moment the best way to check whether you need a stakeholder scheme, or indeed if it really is the best kind of pension, is to log on to the FSA website and click on a decision tree for the stakeholder pension. The website and the phone number are at the end of the chapter.

PERSONAL PENSIONS

Personal pensions were set up for self-employed people who wanted to put money away for old age but did not want to rely on the government pension. Now, though, you can have a personal pension even when you are working for a company.

How is it different from a company pension? Like a company pension, personal pensions are run by a specialised pension company (not the government), but that is the only thing they have in common. When you join your firm's pension scheme you don't pay all the costs of setting up your plan. When you have a personal pension you do have to pay charges and these costs are normally added to your pension payments. In fact when you start a personal pension you may end up paying a lot of money in what are called *upfront charges*.

According to the Financial Services Authority, as many as one person in every four stops paying in within three years. They often then see a large part – sometimes all – of their savings swallowed up by the costs of setting up the plan.

If you are thinking of a personal pension you might be better off going for a stakeholder pension, discussed above. If you already have a personal pension and you want to switch to a stakeholder, beware: you may already have paid the bulk of the personal pension's charges and could lose by switching.

OTHER FORMS OF PENSION

If you have a business you can take advantage of other kinds of personal pension scheme that can do many clever things, such as giving you a loan or allowing you to choose where you invest your contributions. These schemes have funny names such as SSAS (small, self-administered schemes) and EPPs (executive pension plans). These kinds of pensions are normally run by small firms.

SSAS You can't have more than twelve people in a SSAS and you have to have an independent person running the scheme, which means it can be very costly. As with an EPP (see below), cash can be lent back, but there are strict rules on what money can be borrowed for.

EPP Executive pension plans can include just one person or a select few. The benefits can be adjusted to suit each member and half of the pension fund can be lent back.

Self-invested personal pension scheme SIPPS plans are for people who are shrewd enough to work out where they want their pension money to go. Lots of financial gurus such as stockbrokers have SIPPS plans.

Because their job involves their watching stocks and shares, they probably feel well placed to decide where their money goes.

WHAT ELSE IS GOOD ABOUT A PENSION?

If you pay 40 per cent tax you can claim back the same amount of tax on your pension payments. You have to do it yourself, through the self-assessment system – see **Building a Nest**.

But I move around a lot, so is there any point in really having a pension at all? If you really want a pension, and you're not just making excuses, you can set up a portable pension. A number of firms now offer their staff a money-purchase scheme called a *group personal pension* (GPP). This means that your pension money is pooled with other people's, the theory being that the more money there is in the pot, the more you make.

A group personal-pension scheme is the most popular kind of occupational pension because it does allow people to continue putting money into their pension when they change jobs. This is because the pension is yours and not your firm's. With most of these pensions your employer may pay into the plan on your behalf, although these contributions will stop if you change jobs. Also, be aware that special terms your boss may also have negotiated, such as flexible contributions, may be lost if you change jobs.

Ben had a GPP. 'I worked for an Internet firm and they made me redundant,' he says, 'but they'd been quite cool and had given me a good payout. I didn't realise that I could keep running my pension even though I'd left. I'm a bit worried about stuff like that, so knowing I still had a pension and didn't have to set a new one up was good.'

Can I have a private and a company pension? You can, in theory, but you can pay into only one of them – have it 'active' – at any one time. For example, you may have been paying into a private scheme, but decided to start paying into a company scheme. Then your private pension will still exist, but it will be frozen, and your pension money will go into your company scheme.

Can I have a stakeholder at the same time? You can pay into a stakeholder pension only if you are not paying into another pension.

How much can I put into my pension plan? It all depends on your age and the type of pension you have. If you are in your company scheme the most you can put in a year is 15 per cent of your salary.

If you are in a stakeholder scheme or personal-pension plan, you can put in £2,808 a year. This can go up depending on how old you are.

Can I put a lump sum in my pension? Not if it's a company-run scheme – but with some personal pensions you may be able to, so long as the amount you put in doesn't mean your pension contributions go over your allowance.

What if I can't afford to pay into it all of the time? Some personal pensions will let you take 'cash breaks' if, for instance, you are made redundant, have children or move jobs. If you are not in a personal-pension scheme, it may be a bit harder: the larger the scheme, the more inflexible it tends to be. So, if you are in a final-salary pension run by your firm, you may find it tough to take time out. But all pension funds have rules, and yours might be different, so read all the paperwork.

Employers are becoming shrewd because we don't all have jobs for life. If you don't intend to be there a long time you don't have to lose out on having a pension.

I've already got a pension – should I dump it when I start a new job and join my new employer's scheme instead? If you have a personal pension you can freeze it and join your employer's – see above. But this is probably only worth your while if you intend to be there for years, or till you retire. Or you can ask your new firm if you can keep your pension and get them to match your contributions. This is worth asking if they are doing the same for other employees, and the chances are they will ask you if you have a pension already anyway. So, no, don't *automatically* dump your scheme: ask first.

Can I freeze my pension? Yes you can, but remember where it is! Millions of pounds are swimming around in unclaimed pension funds. Lots of people stop and start pensions and then forget about them.

Can I get my money back if I leave? If you have been in a scheme for less than two years you will normally get your money back, minus the bit your firm puts in. When you get the cash you have two options: spend it or transfer it into another pension.

What happens if I transfer it? It depends how much you have. Transferring your pension money can be costly and you may have to fork out charges. The best thing you can do is to get proper advice, as Sandy found out. 'I had £1,000 left over when I got my pension bit back,' said Sandy. 'I was told that if I put it into another pension I wouldn't have to pay any tax – because you only get the tax-free bit if the money is part of a pension.

'I wanted to put the cash into a personal pension but most of the companies I contacted said the minimum they'd take would be two thousand pounds, because transferring money takes up a lot of admin.

'I ended up spending it on a Gucci watch! I suppose I could always sell that if I was short of a few pounds when I get to sixty. After I got the money back it had had income tax taken off it.'

As you've probably realised, there are many risks involving pension transfers, so always seek specialist advice.

I think I'm only putting 5 per cent of my salary into my pension. Is that enough? The consensus seems to be that you should put your maximum amount in, if you can afford it.

Where does my money go? If you work for a big firm, the money you and your colleagues pay towards the pension goes into a big fund called, appropriately enough, a pension fund.

Some companies are so big, like Pearson (the book and newspaper publisher), Marks & Spencer and Shell, that they have their own special pension fund set up. Local authorities, the government, the police force and teachers also have their own special pension funds.

These pension funds are often run by the company itself and the fund has full-time people working to administer it. It also has fund managers and will also pay some outside specialists, such as investment banks and houses, to audit the scheme or act as a consultant when the scheme is being set up or changed. It might for example – and this is very common now – want to change the scheme from a final-salary to a money-purchase one, and will pay a firm to work out the cost.

These pension-fund managers will decide where the money that you pay is invested. Members of pension funds get voting rights, so make sure you use them.

These kinds of pension fund also have trustees, who are there to safeguard the money for the members. If you are putting your money towards the fund, you get a chance to vote on who the trustees are when elections come up.

Smaller companies don't normally have the resources to operate an all-singing, all-dancing pension fund of their own. If they don't, they will normally approach a pension company that specialises in running pensions for medium-sized and smaller firms. When you pay into your company pension you'll still be paying into a pension *fund*, but this fund will be administered out of house.

More often that not these schemes are the money-purchase variety.

Stakeholder schemes and personal pensions are run by pension companies and the money you put in will be invested in things called *unit trusts, shares* and *bonds* – a pick and mix of investments. You may be able to decide what investments your pension cash is put into: some pensions give you an ethical option, for instance, which allows you to make sure your money goes where you want it to.

But you still haven't said where the money actually goes! The pension fund will decide where it thinks the money is best placed to make more for its members – you. Pension funds are the largest investors in stocks and shares in the UK. Pension funds also buy property – the rent goes towards the fund – invest in bonds and gilts and invest in foreign markets and even cash.

Isn't that a bit risky? Shares are always risky investments. That's why pensions also invest in so-called safer places such as bonds. The Pensions Act of 1995 introduced something called a minimum-funding requirement. This means that pension funds always have to have a certain amount of *liquidity* – basically, cold hard cash – so that, if the worst comes to the worst, such as a major economic crisis – people at least get some sort of pension.

Pensions are meant to be long-term investments, so in theory a pension fund should be able to ride the bumps of the investment cycle. But if you retire and it's a bad year you could end up with less of a pension than you expected. One of the reasons final-salary schemes became less popular was because it was proving very expensive and risky to guarantee exactly how much pension someone received.

Even though the value of lots of investments has fallen, pension funds are still the biggest financial forces around. The money put into pensions is so huge that funds can invest in millions of pounds' worth of shares and property (including large property such as shops and office buildings).

The companies in which shares are bought can then use the money to develop new drugs or build new homes. Pension funds are also the largest buyer of government bonds (**How (Maybe) to Make Pots More** has more about these).

So large are pension funds, and such major investors, that, if a pension fund decides to sell all its shares in a company, it can send that company's stock price plummeting. Don't underestimate pensions.

PUMPING UP YOUR PENSION

You can put more cash into your pension but you may have to set up an extra scheme. There are two ways you can do this.

Additional voluntary contributions If you want to put more money into your company pension you are allowed to open a top-up scheme called *additional voluntary contributions* (AVCs). These are not the cheapest way of adding to your pension, but sometimes your firm might chip in as well. If you have a private pension you can increase your contributions. Being in a company scheme can make it more difficult to do that because it is so large.

Free-standing additional voluntary contributions These are often referred to as FSAVCs, and are like AVCs, but you are allowed to decide what the extra money is invested in. Lots of FSAVCs let people invest in ethically minded companies or countries.

What about baby breaks? This is why a lot of women set up AVCs or FSAVCs to boost their pension. This allows them to 'buy years' while they are working.

Will my employer keep paying into my pension if I take maternity leave? They will, but what they pay will depend on what kind of maternity benefits you get. If you are on a reduced pay scale, then your pension payments will be downsized to match that.

PENSION SCANDALS

You can't really talk about pensions without getting the word 'scandal' in there somewhere. If you haven't heard of these three, then you probably need to.

THE MAXWELL SCANDAL: PENSIONS NICKED!

Robert Maxwell was a big newspaper tycoon – big physically as well as being larger than life in other ways – who plundered a pension fund set up for his employees in order to keep afloat ailing parts of his business and to invest in other parts. This huge breach of trust meant that many Maxwell group pensioners ended up with almost nothing.

The reason he was able to do this was because there were no independent trustees – pension guardians – looking after the pension pot. The government introduced several new laws to reassure people that their pensions couldn't be misappropriated in a similar way. This Pensions Act 1995 introduced a safety net, so that if pensions did do badly there was always some cash around. It also allows ordinary pension members to sit on the board of the big pension funds.

THE MISSELLING SCANDAL: SWAPPING GOOD PENSIONS FOR 'BAD'

In the late 1980s and early 1990s financial advisers urged people in perfectly decent private pension schemes to switch their cash into private schemes. Well, lots of company schemes match the pension payments made by the worker (see above). Private schemes don't work like that at all. So people were leaving good schemes to go into ones they had to pay for entirely themselves. This happened because at the time the government was trying to get more people to take out pensions, and also because financial advisers were being paid large commissions by the pension companies. It's all ended up as a bit of a mess, with small financial advisers faced with having to foot the bill for making up the pension cash the people would have had if they had stayed in their old scheme.

The good thing about the misselling scandal is that financial advisers now have to take several exams and if they want to specialise in selling pensions they have to take another exam. The Financial Services Authority also introduced a form of regulation called *compliance*, so all financial advisers have to pay towards their own regulation.

The great thing is that pensions are now, on paper, one of the safest ways to invest your money. If you bought a personal pension between April 1988 June 1994 you may have been a victim of this scam, and should get in touch with the Financial Services Authority.

AND ANOTHER SCANDAL

Equitable Life demonstrated the dangers of promising too much. Thousands of people who took out a pension plan with the company got a shock in the mid-1990s, when they found out they would not be receiving as much cash when they retired as they had been told they would. This then led to legal action as angry customers demanded to get what had been promised to them.

After several years of legal wrangling Equitable Life, which had been a popular choice because it offered cheaper pensions, admitted that low interest rates and falling share prices had slashed the value of the pension fund. According to the BBC's online news website, it now plans to compensate at least 70,000 former pensions and investment customers. Equitable said the total amount of compensation could be in the region of £40 million to £75 million.

Equitable Life has taught the whole world of pensions a few valuable lessons. Here are some that may help.

£   Pension values do go up and down, like the stock market, so beware of companies that offer generous pensions for very little cash.
£   Have other savings to help fund your retirement, such as ISAs or property.
£   Keep an eye on how your pension is doing – you should be getting regular statements telling you exactly how.
£   Don't be afraid to contact your pension company if you do have questions.
£   Look around if you are going to buy a personal pension – the Financial

Services Authority have online comparison tables that track how well pension companies are doing.

£   If you can, find out what the 'free-asset ratio' of your pension company is. This will tell you how much your pension company owes, versus how much if it is worth. If your pension company is worth £10 million, but owes pension payments worth £12 million, then it may not be a good bet. The free-asset ratio tells you how many of its assets are not tied up with paying off people.

PENSION RIGHTS: YOU HAVE TO KNOW

Most pension schemes are called 'trusts'. The trustees are responsible for seeing that the scheme is properly run. You have the right to know about the scheme and information about how your own pension is doing.

We've already looked at the ages at which you can get your pension. The official government retirement age is now 65 for both men and women. But, with a private pension, things are slightly different. Different pension schemes have different retirement ages and as we've seen, some will let you give up work at fifty.

Can I get it any younger? Footballers, firemen, members of the armed services and those in other jobs that give them a limited 'shelf life' are all able to retire early. Because they retire early, they are allowed to put more of their salary into a pension.

So do I get it in a lump sum? You do, but not all of it. If you are in a company scheme you may be entitled to get 25 per cent of your total pension money in a tax-free lump – good for paying off the mortgage or going on a worldwide trek.

If you are in a personal pension you may get an option called *income draw-down* or *income withdrawal*. This means you can take bits of your pension fund from the age of 50 up until you are 75. There are limits on how much you can take, and you still have to buy what is called an annuity.

When your pension money comes through, you can choose to pay yourself an income out of the rest of your pension fund. This means that your pension money becomes a salary to keep you going into your old age. This is done by cashing in your pension, taking your hard-saved cash and then buying what is known as an *annuity*.

An annuity is a product sold by life offices – the people who invest money – to people about to retire. The life office keeps the money and gives it to you monthly or annually, whatever you prefer.

It is a sort of investment product, but you have to buy it all in one go with your pension fund. Think of it as like having thousands of pounds to spend on chocolate for the rest of your life, except that you have to buy it all in one go but are given it monthly or yearly. Well, annuities are a bit like that. The rest of the money that you haven't used – if you've chosen to take 25 per cent of your total fund as a tax-free lump – buys the annuity. If you have built up a fund of £200,000 and taken £50,000 as your lump, then £150,000 is used to buy the annuity.

Does the annuity run out? No, you are paid for the rest of your life, and that's guaranteed. The reason the life offices who sell the annuities can afford to do this is that not everyone lives long enough to use up their annuity income.

Will I know how much I'll get? The price of annuities varies according to how the stock market is performing. If it's an expensive year for annuities, that means it will cost you more to buy your income.

Can I wait till they get cheaper? If you have the luxury of being able to do that, or you can choose to live off your tax-free lump sum, you can wait. But you still have to buy an annuity before the age of 75. There has been a lot of talk about allowing people to buy an annuity whenever they like – because more and more of us are retiring a lot later. If you are not happy with the kind of annuity the life office you bought the pension from is offering you, you have got the chance of shopping around – this is called an *open-market option*.

Is that taxed? Yes, even though you've paid no tax on the pension while you were saving, you do have to pay tax on your new retirement income.

Are there any other ways I can get at my money? Pension companies, innovative souls that they are, introduced something called income draw-down a few years ago. This allows people to start drawing out money from their pension from the age of 55. There are really strict limits on how much you can take out, though.

But wouldn't you run out of money? A lot of people reinvest their income draw-down into other kinds of savings plan. Some do spend it, though, which has worried the government. Normally, when people draw down money in this way, they have to get special advice from a specialist adviser.

Who are actuaries? These are the people who work out the complex pension sums. It's their job to keep up to date with all the latest tax regulations. They are also involved with working out more grisly information such as how much annuities should cost.

What do I pay? Pension companies don't run pensions for free! Managing your money and that of other pension savers is not cheap. In fact the debate about the stakeholder pension centred on the fact that a lot of pension companies felt that they couldn't run such a small pension scheme.

So where do my charges go?

To **fund managers**. These are the people who make strategic decisions about what the pension fund should be investing in to make more money. They will be constantly monitoring new trends, such as share and bond prices.

To **stockbrokers**. These are the people you buy the shares from – they take a cut from every share sold, and this is how they make their money.

And to **other** people such as admin staff and the financial adviser who sells you the pension.

And how are these paid? Whether you are in a personal pension or a company scheme there are a number of charges you'll have to pay.

Upfront charges These are all taken out when you start paying into the pension, but you can with some companies choose to spread them. The upfront charges will cover the costs above. In a personal or stakeholder pension, you foot the bill for the charges and, although you may have to pay some charges if you join a company scheme, they will not be as much because the pension is already set up.

Personal pensions are notorious for charging high upfront costs; stakeholder pensions are normally cheaper.

Management charges These are charges that are paid to the fund managers and those who decide the best investments for the pension fund.

Commission If you have bought a personal pension through a financial adviser they will take a payment known as commission. This depends on how much you pay into the pension.

Do I still have to pay if I think the pension isn't being run properly? It's that old word 'risk' again. Pensions are investment products. But if a firm feels that its pension isn't being run properly it can sack the fund-management firm or manager running the fund. This doesn't happen often but when it does it tends to hit the headlines.

Are pensions one big tax dodge? So much regulation surrounds pensions, especially on tax, that they can look like one big tax dodge for rich people and an unnecessary expense for ordinary people.

Do pensions always do well? Pensions have their rough times. They do, after all, rely on stocks and shares, and falls in the stock market mean they may go through rocky patches. That's why you need to keep an eye on how your cash is doing.

So is it worth my investing in one? If you are in a final-salary scheme you need not worry at all because you'll get a percentage of your salary and not how much you've saved.

Can I be more active in my pension? If you wish, you can be like Brett and take more notice of what your pension is invested in. 'I took out a group personal pension through work,' he says, 'and I kept getting lots of booklets asking me how I was going to invest my money. I never really saw my pension as an investment, but it was when one of my friends recommended that I had a good look at where my money really was going that I actually got into it. You have to remember that your money as a pension person is being used to invest in lots of things.

'I started paying attention to all the financial newspapers, and I even started to look and see how the FTSE was doing on the news every night. I turned from being a passive investor to an active one.'

What do fund managers do when the going gets tough? When things get tough in a pension fund the investment managers put money away from shares and into other forms of investment such as bonds and gilts. There is more information about these in **How (Maybe) to Make Pots More**.

OTHER WAYS TO A RICH(ER) OLD AGE

It's not just about pensions: there are other ways of making sure that your exotic holidays remain an annual event when you get older.

NICER ISAS

Yes, those handy little savings accounts (see **Saving**) are not such a small deal. If you save £3,000 each year in a cash ISA you can build yourself up a nice little sum. Or you can go the whole hog and stick £7,000 in a maxi version.

The only cons with ISAs is that the government has guaranteed their existence only until 2006. As with PEPS and TESSAs, it's likely they will have a limited shelf life. You can keep them going, but you won't be able to keep putting money into them. Then again the popularity of these tax-free savings schemes has been such that they probably will be replaced with something else. It could even be something better.

Pros and cons Well, you don't pay tax, but ISAs are risky. Shares – here we go again – are subject to rocky rides as much as property is, but, that said, if you are prepared to hold on to them for decades you could end up with a nice little money pot.

PAYING OFF PROPERTY

With some careful planning, you could aim to have paid off your mortgage, which would mean that the only things you have to fork out for are living expenses. You could also invest in other property. As Vicki said earlier, 'My mum and dad have both got a third each of my flat – they've said that that is their retirement income.'

Pros and cons Property does do quite well but, as with shares, it can be difficult to gauge when to sell and when to buy. You are always going to be taking some risk – pension funds tend to have 6 per cent of their cash invested in property-type investments.

WHERE DO I BUY A PENSION?

Buying a pension is easier now than ever. Some pension companies even operate over the Internet – although, because they are complicated beasts, nearly all firms will want you to go over the finer points of your retirement plans with one of their advisers, face to face or over the phone. If you want to look around for a pension, it would be best for you to speak to an independent financial adviser. You can find local pension experts by calling the IFA Promotion hotline (see **Resources**). They can put you in touch with advisers who specialise in pensions.

What should I be looking for?

Security First, is the company you're buying the pension from a secure concern? Nearly all pension companies are regulated by the Financial Services Authority. There are a few exceptions: people with executive pension schemes sometimes take out offshore-based pensions, for instance. If the company you are buying the pension from is based in the UK you will have some protection from the FSA.

Pension companies do change and buy each other out, but because your pension is for a long time it's a good idea to make sure your investment is in the best possible hands. Even if the company offering you a pension does go belly up, you are protected if its regulated by the FSA.

Can I get my money back? If you've been paying into a personal pension you may have to kiss the money *adieu* until you retire. If you are with a company scheme you'll be able to get your money back only if you want to leave the company. Bear in mind that different pension schemes have different rules.

HOW TO PLAN FOR RETIREMENT

Still flummoxed by all this talk? Read this checklist and be afraid no longer:

£   When? What age do you want to retire?
£   How much? On what kind of money do you want to retire?
£   Can you afford it? You'll be paying into it every month, remember.
£   Do you want to stop? Make sure you get a flexible pension that allows you to stop paying in.
£   Do you want to add to it? You may have save extra if you want to take time off to start a family.
£   Do you have one already? Where are your other pensions? Make sure you know.
£   What else have you got? Property, ISAs, even other savings can help you to a richer retirement.
£   Investing? Why not be more risky with your money?

I don't know where my previous company pension is If you've lost track of any pensions you may have had with a previous employer, the Pension Schemes Registry may be able to help you (see **Resources** for contact details for OPRA).

Is it too late to start a pension? Pension companies and the media have been painting a dire picture of people who haven't taken out their first pension almost before they leave school! It is true that the more cash you do stash away, and the younger you are when you start doing it, the more you should get when you retire. But, even if you've reached your thirties and spent nearly all your cash on having a good time, it doesn't mean it's too late to start a pension. Remember, though, when you read the next scare story about pension companies, that, yes, you do need to put something by – in fact something is better than nothing at all.

Can I really afford a pension? Suppose you are, say, in your thirties and all your available money is going on your mortgage, perhaps you haven't got fifty pounds to spare towards a pension. Well, you may be best starting a stakeholder scheme, into which you can put as little as £25 a month. You can always increase that amount when you find yourself with some spare cash.

Should I really be joining my firm's scheme, especially if I'm not going to be there for very long? Yes, you probably, note probably, should be joining your work scheme. Being part of a large pension scheme means you get lots of benefits, and your employer is putting money in for you as well.

TALES FROM THE UNEXPECTED

So you think your parents, uncles, aunts and grandparents have been so sensible. Here are a few words of pension wisdom.

'My stepdaughter started a pension when she was twenty-four. I didn't start mine till I was fifty!' says Jennifer. 'There are other ways of making sure that you do have some money. I intend to sell my house and downsize to a smaller place. I didn't tell her that. I made some very unwise money decisions in my time and I wanted to encourage her to take out some kind of retirement provision.'

'My father paid off his mortgage when he was forty-eight,' says Marianne. 'All the disposable income he had then went into his pension. He had hardly paid anything into it [before] because he'd be bringing up five children.

Jo also left it until later. 'When my son went to university we started putting a thousand pounds into our pension to make up for lost time. Now that really seems like a lot but we had paid off our mortgage and we had managed to save up for our son's fees. So we did have extra cash.'

'I have no pension at all, it scares the living daylights out of me,' says Kim. 'I'm not relying on my children to help. I'm fifty-eight and the only thing I really have is my house.'

PENSIONS OF THE FUTURE?

DO-IT-YOURSELF PENSIONS

A few years ago it was really only the really, really rich who chose where their pension money was invested. These self-invested personal-pension schemes, or SIPPS plans – see earlier – were, and still are, popular with senior executives. But now, thanks to what companies call investor awareness, more of us want to decide where our pension cash goes.

The Maxwell scandal did much to publicise what happens when people paying into a pension don't know what their money is up to. There's also been a growing empowerment as everyone begins to realise that they can try to make a difference. The growth of ethical funds (see **How (Maybe) To Make Pots More**), where people actively choose not to invest their cash in companies with questionable environmental, political and ethical practices, has kick-started the trend.

But you don't have to be ethically minded to want to decide where your cash goes. Pension companies now offer self-select pensions. You don't choose individual shares but you can decide what kinds of companies or investments your cash will be spent on.

This requires some homework. For basic investment information read **How (Maybe) to Make Pots More**. The kinds of things that you can invest in may include overseas companies that invest in small companies, or the more general small UK stocks.

'My firm has a group personal pension with Friends Provident,' says Lauren. 'When we were asked if we wanted to join the pension we were given a booklet explaining all the different kinds of funds. At the time the stock market wasn't doing so well – and even I knew it would be better to put my money into somewhere a bit more general.'

RETIREMENT AGE

This isn't strictly a money issue but it's nearly always coming up in the news. We are becoming fitter and healthier than our grandparents, but this could also have repercussions for our retirement age.

Pension funds are running out of money, so we may have to work longer, or opt to retire later – retiring early may be an option only if we have put more money into our pension pots when we were young.

The government scheme may no longer exist – this may mean that it may become compulsory for us to put money into a private pension.

In the future, retirement may not be allowed until eighty, but this will depend on what happens to the population. If the birth rate falls, there will be fewer people in work paying taxes and National Insurance contributions.

ANNUITIES

Pensions themselves may have to adjust. There may be an extension to the age at which people have to buy annuities. In fact there may be no restrictions at all, which means that, instead of having to buy an income, pensioners can keep drawing down their pension as cash – although this will have to be taxed. This means that we may be able to keep investing our money, something an annuity stops us from doing. Pensions may become more expensive – some pensions may start offering healthcare as an extra because, as we live longer, the chances are we may find ourselves needing more help in that direction.

PENSION SPLITTING

When a couple are divorced there may be cases where the wife is entitled to a share of the pension fund her husband has built up. This will happen if the wife has not been able to work – because, maybe, she has been staying at home to bring up children. If this happens, a court can decide to split the pension, or the part that was paid into the pension while the couple were together.

If the couple become divorced before they retire, the pension fund can be earmarked. This means that the bit of pension cash built up while they were married is put into another fund. This is so that the couple don't have to keep in contact in order to make sure their pensions are sorted out. Pensions are now considered an asset under divorce settlements.

WITH-PROFITS PENSIONS

These are a particular type of pension that has been doing quite well over the last twenty years. They are not easy to understand, though, and that's why the Financial Services Authority is looking at making them more transparent to the public.

If you invest in a with-profits pension – these are normally offered only by insurance companies and friendly societies – you will get bonuses in return. These are in addition to reversionary, or regular, bonuses that you may get once a year. And at the end of your investment, when your money is turned into a pension, you receive a terminal bonus.

Bonuses do vary from year to year, and sometimes, especially if a company reckons it's going to face a tough year ahead, it may keep back bonuses. This means it saves money that allows it to smooth over the bad years.

INTERNET PENSIONS

A lot of banks already offer Internet-based stakeholder pensions. If you have one you'll already know that you can look up your details and check the performance of your pension cash. At the moment you can't actually set up a pension on the Internet: it normally has to be done through your firm. Soon it may be possible for all of us to check our pensions with a few mouse clicks. Now that would be interesting.

MORE HELP FOR YOU

Here are some useful addresses for those who want to know more. By the way, pensions are tough nuts to crack, and, if you really are unsure about what's best for you, contact a specialist pensions adviser. IFA Promotion (details in **Resources**) will be able to find up to three suitable ones in your area who know pensions inside out.

The Department for Work and Pensions has a helpline on 08457 31 32 33 for guides on pensions.

The Office for the Pensions Advisory Service (OPAS) gives advice on all aspects of company pensions. You can also complain to them about your scheme on 0845 6012923 or write to them at 11 Belgrave Road, London SW1V 1RB. Their website is at www.opas.org.uk.

The Financial Services Authority (see **Resources**) can help you if you feel you have been missold a pension. It also has online comparison tables to help you decide which pension company is offering the best deal.

Pension protection If you think your company pension scheme is not doing all it should be to keep you informed you can contact the

Occupational Pensions Regulatory Authority (OPRA) on 01273 627600, or at www.opra.gov.uk.

Stakeholder information If your firm has more than five staff and you don't have a stakeholder pension scheme, contact the OPAS Stakeholder Pensions Hotline through the website www.stakeholderhelpline.org.uk or on 08456 012 923.

9 HOW (MAYBE) TO MAKE POTS MORE

Did you spot the heading of this chapter and decide to skip the rest of the book to get to this bit? If so, be warned: making more money, aside from your usual day job, is no easy ride. If you haven't looked at it first, then retrace your steps immediately to **Saving**, because putting your cash into shares, unit trusts, bonds and suchlike can be scary and frustrating. The chances are, too, that it'll dig a deep hole into your wallet before it makes you rich.

There are many different ways to invest your money if you are willing to take the risk.

£   **Grab a share.** You can pick out companies that you reckon will be the next big thing, and then buy shares in them, although doing some prior homework is always advisable.
£   **Go a bundle.** You can go for a bundle of shares and spread your risk by buying collective investments such as unit trusts, investment trusts and OEICs (which stands for open-ended investment companies).
£   **Extra risk.** You could be extra risky and buy bonds that invest in just one company, or even single shares.
£   **The safe option.** Or you could play it safe and go for something that buys up so-called secure savings such as government bonds.
£   **Or just gamble.** Then of course there are the derivatives-based investments such as futures, where you don't buy shares, but instead gamble on what you reckon the share's price will be in the future.

Warning: investing in the stock market, or just about anything share-based, is risky.

SHARES – GETTING YOUR SLICE OF A COMPANY

Whether they are doing badly, brilliantly or just in the doldrums, shares are the building blocks of nearly all investments. You've already seen how pensions and even ISAs use shares.

'The first I knew about shares was when I was nineteen,' Simon confides, 'and there were all the ads for [the privatisation of] British Gas asking where "Sid" was. This was in the mid-1980s, I think. Margaret Thatcher and her government wanted to change the ownership of all the public companies so that they were owned by shareholders. The idea was that they were able to raise money, make more people own shares and of course save the government having to spend a lot of money propping up public utilities.'

Not everyone may have agreed with Margaret Thatcher's attempt to privatise companies such as British Gas and British Telecom, but the Iron Lady did leave one legacy behind: she turned the public into share-crazed investors.

When the shares for British Gas went on sale they were snapped up. And a lot of people made good money selling the shares they had preordered (this in share-speak is called being 'subscribed to'). People who had never even shaken a stick at the stock market suddenly started becoming interested in what shares, or what *their* shares, were doing.

So below is a more in-depth look at shares, where to find them, what sort of companies have them, how to find them and why people buy them.

What are shares? Think of a company as being like a large cake divided up into bits, but instead of having eight pieces it has more like millions and millions of bits. Each share may cost only about £10, but when you put the cost of all the shares together you get an awful lot of money. The value of all the shares added together is known as that company's *market capitalisation*.

When you buy a share you are buying a very, very small bit of a company – most UK companies have thousands of shareholders.

Do all companies have shares? No, you'll know whether a company has shareholders or not because it will have the initials 'PLC' after its name: this means the company is a public limited company.

Privately owned companies, those that tend to be owned by only a director and a few other founders or other managers, are called *limited companies*. Limited companies do have shares but they cannot be publicly bought.

Where are shares? Companies with shareholders have a listing on the London Stock Exchange. This is like the central clearing house

– a kind of bank – for shares, if you like. LSE, as it's known, used to be based in a building in the City – in Leadenhall Street – and that is where all share dealing was done. Now, though, it's all done via computer.

Finding your share In the LSE there are lots of different subcategories that allow people to look quickly for the kinds of shares they want. The FTSE 100 (in full: the *Financial Times* Stock Exchange 100 Index; often called 'the Footsie') is the bit of the stock exchange that lists the top 100 shareholder-owned companies in the UK. The FTSE 250 lists the next largest companies *including* the top 100, and the FTSE 500 lists the 500 largest companies.

The Stock Exchange is responsible for setting up and managing the computerised system that allows people to deal with shares. It is not responsible for making sure that shares are sold properly: that is the job of the Financial Services Authority.

What about non-UK companies? You can still buy the shares of companies that are based abroad – it's just that they are listed on different stock exchanges. An American company, for example, will be listed on the New York Stock Exchange in Wall Street; instead of being called the FTSE, it's the Dow Jones, or NASDAQ if it's a technology company. The Japanese stock exchange is called the Nikkei and the French is called the CACI. If you live in the UK you can buy shares of foreign companies, but you'll get taxed here.

Why do people buy shares?

Shares used to be a way of making a quick buck. People today buy shares because over years and years they do tend to make a bit of money. A lot of very rich people buy shares and then sell them over short periods of time. This can make money, especially if you buy quite a few, because share prices do go up and down. If you buy them when they are cheap and then sell then when they are expensive, you can make quite a bit, but you may have to pay capital gains tax if you make more money than your personal allowance (**A Little Bit of Protection** has more about this).

A lot of the shares bought on the London Stock Exchange are bought by big institutions on behalf of their clients, who can be individuals like you or large investors such as pension funds. Or they can be bought, in some cases, by companies wanting to bag themselves shares in another company. Shares can also be a way for one company to buy into or take over another: if they buy enough shares then they can wangle their way on to the board of the company they are buying up. There are strict rules about this, though, and, if one company does start buying up lots of shares in another, it can no longer remain anonymous.

Why do companies have shares? Shares can be a way of raising money and for rewarding those who have invested money. People with shares get paid a dividend, sometimes only a few pence, for each share they have. If a company wants to raise money to invest in new buildings, new staff or new technology it has the option of being able to issue more shares. If a company is not doing so well a large share issue aimed at raising large amounts of cash may backfire, because the increased availability of shares will make the current ones less desirable, and worth less. Before issuing more shares a company will normally consider the effect on its existing shareholders.

How do you know what shares to buy? You don't. Even experts make mistakes. In 1999 and 2000 technology and Internet shares soared to incredible highs, only to drop dramatically. Even seasoned market watchers, people who buy shares for a living, such as stockbrokers and fund mangers, bought up thousands of these shares only to lose out when they dropped.

Of course, most of the time, buying shares is a bit more lucrative. If you are not sure what to buy, keep your eye on newspapers, look out for the latest company reports and keep an eye on trends.

How do you know when to sell a share? You never really know when to sell a share. All sorts of things can make share prices go up and down, and dramatic falls and rises can happen over just one day. The best thing may be to buy a share in a company that you like.

Jacqui explains how she bought her first shares: 'I spend a lot of money in Oasis and Marks & Spencer. When I got a bonus at work I promised myself that I would start buying shares. So I thought, Where do I spend most of my money? And that's when I thought it would be good to actually get something, even a small bit, out of the companies where I spend loads of cash.

'I've also bought shares in Coffee Republic because I love their coffee, although they are not doing so well at the moment.

'I'm always taking Marks & Spencer food to picnics and now I notice my friends are all starting to shop there, too. So I'm getting more money back.'

The late Victor Kiam bought the electric-shaver company Remington because he liked the product so much (remember the TV adverts?). If you do have a passion for something, remember that you as a consumer are probably not the only one to like the brand.

Sasha also buys shares in companies she likes: 'I guess I got to be a real spod and loads of my clothes are from Oasis. All my mates see me in clothes I like and that make me feel good so they often buy the odd thing in there. Of course, you could get more scientific about your choice of shares.'

'I reckon medicine is going to be the next big thing,' says Caroline, a new investor. 'A lot of the pharmaceutical companies are making breakthroughs with medicines that could change the world. Look at the news that pigs have been cloned to produce transplant organs that don't get rejected. I've got a portfolio of stocks that spreads across pharmaceuticals – that's what the medical companies are known as.'

What's the fallout theory? This is when certain things pick up and other industries are set to benefit from them. You might get the fallout stocks cheaper because the immediate effect hasn't caught on yet.

For example, computer firms did well when the Internet took off but it was a while before companies that made computer parts did well – the semiconductor companies and those that made computer chips started to pick up later.

So what are the tricks? Pick a stock that's on its way up, but don't believe all the hype you read in the papers: go with your instinct. Pick something that you enjoy. Remember: you're going to be constantly monitoring the price of your stock, so it's got to be something that gets you going.

Have fun Don't invest too much to start with, give yourself a 'gambling' budget of about £100. Natalie wishes she had done just that. 'My friend had a tip-off about some stocks,' she says. 'I won't say which ones. I put three thousand pounds into them, just one company, only to see the value drop right down. I should have started with a smaller amount, and then, if it had done well, I could have put the rest of my cash in.'

What about share falls? Shares are becoming much more of a long-term investment. And to make money you have to be prepared to hold on to them for a while.

Where do I buy shares? The main people licensed to sell and buy shares are called *stockbrokers*. To work as a stockbroker you have to take a series of exams. Stockbrokers are also known as *private client investment managers* and can also work within the investment parts of banks, where they are often known as *analysts*.

Stockbrokers are also companies or individuals who make money from the buying and selling of shares.

There are three different types of stockbroker and how much money they charge depends on how hands-on their service is.

Execution-only stockbrokers These are the stockbrokers who act on your orders. You ask them to buy the shares and that's what they do. They don't offer advice and are the cheapest place to get shares.

Sam says, 'When I first bought shares I did it through my bank. All I had to do was decide what shares to buy. They then charged me a fee. I bought a hundred pounds' worth of shares and paid twenty-five pounds on top of that.'

Nearly all the banks have a stockbroking arm that allows you to buy shares on the phone or even on the Internet. Some stockbrokers have set up Internet sites that allow you to buy shares without paying a fee.

Steven, an editor, said, 'I bought my shares over the Internet. They were offering a special deal where you didn't pay any fees for your first few transactions.'

Advisory stockbrokers These stockbrokers recommend which shares to buy and sell. First, though, they'll work out what sort of companies are the best ones for you to buy into. From time to time they may also get in touch with you about other shares you may be interested in.

Discretionary stockbrokers, also known as private client investment managers These are stockbrokers employed by richer people and will be given carte blanche to buy the shares they think will make their clients money. These stockbrokers operate at what is called the 'top end' of the market. Very wealthy people who can afford to will often employ their own stockbroker.

Vicki sees first hand what goes on at a stockbroker's: 'I work as an assistant in a stockbroking firm. It's my responsibility to keep ahead of the market and decide what stocks are on the up. The stockbrokers in the firm buy up the shares without having to ask their clients' permission.'

Dealing on the Net Internet share dealing is cheaper, because the stockbroker doesn't have to pay the same kind of overheads as an office-based firm. An Internet-based stockbroker will nearly always be an execution-only one. Someone doing business with an Internet stockbroker will be protected by the same rules as if they had done business over the phone or face to face. If you want a list of stock brokers contact the Association of Private Client Investment Managers.

DIFFERENT STAGES OF BUYING SHARES

The *initial public offering* is when the company is first listed on the stock exchange. This is also called the *flotation* and is when you can buy the shares in advance. If you find out a company is floating and you want to buy shares in advance you can contact the London Stock Exchange to find out when the shares will be on sale and then let your stockbroker know you want to buy them. After the flotation a company may issue further shares – this is called a *further issue*. But the most common way of buying shares is through day-to-day selling, often called *trading market*.

How do I find out the price of a share?

The prices of shares are listed in the *Financial Times* and you can normally get the price of the top-100 shares (the FTSE 100) in the financial and business pages of all national newspapers. These prices relate to what the share was worth on the previous day. The share prices will appear in a table and, as well as the current price of the share, the table will show you the lowest and highest prices that share has achieved during that year. To get up-to-the-minute share prices you can check online at www.ft.com or on the London Stock Exchange's website, listed below. If you are in a bank you may be able to check the price on a computer system known as Market Eye, but your bank branch has to have what is known as a ShareShop. This also has company information.

What do I pay for shares? When you buy your shares you pay your stockbroker. What you pay when you buy your shares depends on what kind of stockbroker you use. The more advice the stockbroker gives you on what shares to buy, the more you will pay. As a rule an execution-only service is the cheapest and a discretionary service will be the most expensive.

You need to check with your stockbroker first and it's a good idea – as with everything else – to compare the charges of different stockbrokers before you decide to do business with one. All stockbrokers charge a minimum commission, but others may include other charges, and there may be some ongoing costs too every time you buy or sell your shares. Remember that all these charges are *on top of* the price of the shares.

There's also a tax (mentioned earlier) – stamp duty – that you pay when you buy shares, though not when you sell them. This works out at about 0.5 per cent of the price of each share – so if you buy £20 worth of shares you'll pay 10p of tax on top.

Do I see the shares? When you buy shares you can hold them in a share account – which is all electronic. You also get share certificates, which are bits of paper confirming you are a shareholder.

Why nothing is free, especially not when it comes to finance

Finance companies have to make their cash somehow, and they normally do it through a series of charges. These charges differ depending on what kind of investment you choose, but there are also different kinds of charges: sometimes you end up paying not one but a couple of charges – ISAs, for example, may have an annual charge and an initial charge.

Popular charges to look out for:

£ **Initial, or upfront, charge – this is the charge that you pay at the start of your investment. It can be a one-off fee or part of a charging structure that also involves paying a regular charge as well (see below). Personal pensions tend to have the highest initial charges.**

£ **Annual charge/management fee – this is a regular charge that financial companies make to pay for the costs involved in managing your money, such as paying for fund managers. The more complex the financial product you are buying – for example, a unit trust where daily decisions are made about where to switch your cash – the more of these charges you tend to have to pay.**

It also depends whether you buy your product through a financial adviser. Most advisers get paid commission (paid to them out of the charges you pay). They may forego commission, though, and charge an upfront fee, which may mean that the financial product you buy ends up being cheaper – advisers make more money the longer you keep investing.

Remember that different companies have different charging structures, but you have every right to ask exactly how much, and how often, you will be charged. And if you think you are being charged too much – you probably are.

What else do I get? As a shareholder you also have other entitlements such as the right to vote at the company's annual meeting and you should get regular company reports.

If you so choose, you can allow your stockbroker to keep your shares in an electronic account, called a *nominee account*. This means that the stockbroker looks after the running of your shares. This may cost more, though.

Most people don't like the idea of buying shares on their own. That's why financial companies have started to offer packages of shares or collective investments. This means you can buy into a number of different companies and spread your risk.

SPREADING YOUR RISK – BUYING LOTS OF SHARES WITHOUT SO MUCH WORRY

If you want to spread your risk, there are ways of buying lots of shares in different companies.

Collective investments As you have seen in **Saving**, stocks-and-shares ISAs allow you to invest £7,000 a year tax free. Still, if you are lucky enough to have used your ISA allowance for the year, you may still be ready to put your cash into other investments, if:

£   you've got more than £100 to invest, and you want to have fun (or give yourself the willies!)
£   you want to learn more about the stock market
£   you fancy going it alone
£   you want to set up a share club (see below)

Collective investments come in several different forms. They are not too difficult to understand and the main difference between them tends to be how they invest and how the shares are bundled up.

These kinds of investment are seen as safer than shares alone because they also invest in other areas, such as bonds. This is normally done to give investors a safety net in case the shares do really badly.

Unit trusts When you put your money into a unit trust you are not buying a share: you are buying a unit.

Unit trusts are normally themed groups of shares: you can get a unit trust that has the shares of smaller UK companies, for instance, or one that invests in, say, Latin America. You can also have unit trusts that invest only in companies with ethical practices.

You can put your money into a unit trust monthly, as with a savings account, or annually.

The fund gets bigger as more people invest in it; if a lot of people start to take their money out the fund becomes smaller. The more people who want to invest in a unit trust, the more expensive each unit is. So, like good-quality chocolate or a pair of designer shoes, the more the trust is worth, the more you have to pay to put money into it. The technical name for a unit trust is an *open-ended fund*, because there is no limit on the number of people who can invest in it.

Like a pension fund, a unit trust has someone to manage all the investments and make sure investors like you are getting the most from your cash.

What are investment trusts? Investment trusts are set up like companies, so they actually have their own listing on the London Stock Exchange (under 'investment trusts').

They work like any other company, but they make money by investing in other companies, and not by selling goods. Like unit trusts, they have themes: an investment trust may specialise, for example in emerging markets or smaller UK companies.

Unlike a unit trust, what you are buying is an actual share, and you can also invest in an investment trust as part of your ISA allowance.

Investment trusts are called *closed-ended funds*, because there are only so many shares per trust. This is why investment trusts are advertised sometimes as limited offers.

How much does it cost? The shares in an investment fund will depend on the value of the companies it invests in. If you've got a fund investing in technology, and then technology shares fall, then the investment funds that invest in technology shares will also fall.

It also works like supply and demand as well. If lots of people want to buy shares but not many people want to sell them, the price of the shares can go up. If there are more people wishing to sell than wishing to buy, the share price tends to fall.

Investment trusts are also allowed to borrow money to buy other shares, which gives them an extra risk element: if the investment trust makes a bad investment itself, your shares will be worth less. Unlike unit trusts, investment trust have different types of shares:

£   income shares, which pay out an income like a salary
£   growth shares, where the money the shares make is put back into the trust and you can't get at it until you take all your cash out

What do I pay for unit trusts and investment trusts? You have to pay an initial charge to the investment trust company when you buy a unit trust. Some unit trusts don't make this charge, but that doesn't mean that your unit trust is cheaper – a lot of unit trusts charge an exit charge when you take your money out, and nearly all unit trusts include a management charge.

Investment trusts have a more complicated pricing deal than unit trusts because you are buying shares. You usually pay charges when you buy and sell investment-trust shares, and you also pay a yearly management fee.

Remember, though, that nothing is free in the world of finance – see the box on charging for shares (above) for some reminders of what to look out for and check when it comes to charges on investments.

How much can I save? With both unit and investment trusts you can save monthly. Most will expect you to pay a minimum of £50 per month, or you can put in a lump sum and add to it when you get more cash.

What are OEICs? Or are they oiks? These are *open-ended investment companies*, or OEICs. And, yes, it's pronounced 'oiks'. These haven't been around that long, but don't let the name put you off. OEICs are a hybrid of unit and investment trusts.

How does an OEIC work? An OEIC is a company that manages other investments, like an investment trust. But, unlike the case with an investment trust, there is no limit to the number of shares. That is why, like a unit trust, it is an open-ended investment.

This means if more people buy the shares of an OEIC, the fund grows, and more shares are created. Then again, if it gets smaller and people take their money out, the fund shrinks. The better the investments in the fund do, the more the shares are worth.

What do you pay? You usually pay an initial charge when you buy and sell OEIC shares – this is the same as you would pay when buying and selling shares.

Not all OEICs have an initial charge but you may have to pay what is known as an *exit charge*, and you will most certainly have to pay a yearly management fee.

Why should I buy an OEIC? OEICs are not as popular as unit trusts or investment trusts but, as with those two, you can choose to pay monthly or invest a lump sum. The pricing is supposed to be easier to understand.

HIGH-RISK INVESTMENTS

In case your appetite is whetted here are a few more investments. Be warned: all of these are risky, but if you do fancy gambling your money read on.

EXCHANGE-TRADED FUNDS

These are like shares. All ETFs, as they are known, are listed on the stock market. They buy shares and make their money by tracking an index. It can be a stock market one, such as the FTSE 100, or it can be a sector, such as European pharmaceutical firms.

The ETF is open-ended, like a unit trust. The bigger the fund – the more money invested – the more the share is worth. You make money in the form of a dividend if the index does well, or you can sell your shares when their value goes up. You can normally put in only a lump sum, though.

Charges You pay stockbroker's commission when you buy and sell, and a management charge. But, unlike the case with other shares, there is no stamp duty to pay on purchases.

SO MANY FUNDS, SO LITTLE TIME

Unit trusts, investment trusts and OEICs don't invest only in shares. They may also include some/all of the following.

£ **Money market: These are cash deposits – they are safe but they don't tend to pay much interest.**

£ **Bonds: This is when the investment buys corporate bonds (for bond descriptions see below) and gilts. These are not very risky, either.**

£ **Tracker: These funds move in line with a selected stock market index such as the FTSE 100. They can be quite risky.**

£ **Specialist: These are high-risk because they concentrate on one small thing such as shares in Latin American or Asian companies.**

£ **Ethical: These are investments that refuse to put their money into companies that have unethical or environmentally unfriendly policies.**

HOW YOU GET YOUR MONEY

When you take out an investment, of whatever kind, you may be asked to choose how you want to be paid your interest.

Income Some investments will pay you an income. This means that, when your money has made money, the interest is paid into your bank account yearly or in some cases monthly.

Growth Others, normally with the word 'growth' in them, will not give you any money until your investment matures, or you ask for your money back.

High-income investments: a warning All investments are risky, but be especially aware before you decide to put your cash into an investment offering high income. The word 'income' makes the whole thing sound safe and secure, but it's not. These things can be dangerous. You might not get back the money you put in (the capital). The better the offer seems, the more risky it is. Often, you have to put your money away for a while and it may achieve a high income only if certain conditions are met. You can get high-income bonds (these are the ones that invest in companies), unit trusts and even ISAs. **Always read the small print if you are tempted to go for one of these**.

CHECK YOUR INTEREST, TOO!

How your interest is calculated varies and it may not always take into account what you originally put in.

What happens if the investment fund I'm with loses money? Some funds will guarantee that you get your initial capital back, whatever happens. But if things go seriously wrong that may not always be the case. You may be able to claim compensation if you can prove the investment company has been negligent with your cash. If you think this has happened contact the Financial Services Authority.

Is it possible to get rich quickly? It used to be a lot easier to make money on the stock market in a matter of hours. In fact it used to be *very* easy – people used to buy and sell shares overnight to make a profit. This was known as *bed-and-breakfasting*. It's not so popular any more because the government introduced tax laws to stop it.

The Internet boom extended beyond Internet stocks themselves to trading on the Internet. Day traders in America became a whole new industry, making lots of cash by sitting all day picking stocks off the Internet; but, with the fall in the prices of shares, these days are long gone.

You can still buy and sell shares over a short period of time. Whether you make any money in that time ... well, it's pretty risky.

'My boyfriend was convinced he could make money buying and selling shares on the Internet,' says Tanya. 'So he gave up his job, leaving me to bring home the money for the mortgage. He bought himself a computer and spent all day trading using stockbroker and share-buying sites. He lost over two thousand pounds in a month.'

Having the guts to buy shares and making wise buys is a matter of chance. Not everyone has it in them to be an investment guru. In which case there are other, safer, ways of taking a bet with your money.

INVESTMENT TERMS

You may have come across a number of terms, both in this book so far and in the financial stories in your daily paper or on TV or radio.

So let us look at what 'bonds' and 'gilts' are, along with 'with-profits products' and 'share clubs'.

Gilts (also called government bonds) Think of gilts as being like a loan to the government. When the government sells gilts it's trying to raise money. When you buy a gilt you get a guarantee of receiving interest back, normally a couple of times a year, on your investment. Gilts are not for life, though: the government will agree to buy the gilt back from you on a specific date. It could be three years or it could be ten (well, you don't think they'd want to keep paying you interest for ever, do you?).

Gilts are not cheap: they come in multiples of at least £100 and, if you buy them through a bank or stockbroker, you normally have to put up at least £2,000.

When interest rates and/or share prices are low, gilts may look more attractive to people wanting to invest their cash.

How do you buy and sell gilts? You can buy them through a firm offering stockbroking services. You will pay commission charges for this service, as when buying other investments in this way.

Are they risky? No, they are thought to be one of the safest stock market investments.

Bonds Bonds are like gilts, except that they are issued by companies wanting to raise money. They, too, are for a limited period and agree to pay you a rate of interest that is fixed right at the beginning. They are more risky than government bonds, because, if the company issuing the bond goes out of business, you may not get all your cash back. Bonds can be bought through stockbrokers and you also pay commission.

When is a bond not a bond? Lots of banks and building societies offer products called *guaranteed bonds*. In most cases these are investment schemes that pay you regular interest as income. Very often the bond may be a way for the bank to raise money. The word 'guaranteed' normally means, unless the product specifies otherwise, that you are entitled to get back the original amount you invested. Remember that different banks use the word 'guarantee' differently, so check the small print first.

With-profits With-profits products, whether they are bonds or funds, mean that any money you make is based on the success of the company you are investing in. You can get with-profits endowments and pensions. The with-profits title means that you get a bonus for each year you have the investment (though remember that a bonus is just that; it's not a guaranteed payment), and very often a terminal bonus when the investment matures (usually after 25 years). Think carefully before you take out a with-profits investment. Or, better still, get expert advice.

DIVIDEND

This is, if you like, the profit made by a share. Once a year a company will announce, normally at its annual general meeting, how much money it plans to distribute among its shareholders. The dividend is paid per share and is normally only a few pence.

SHARE CLUBS

These are funky little groups that make share buying a little more sociable and fun, as long as you can agree what shares you want to buy.

'We set up a share club at the gym,' says Margaret. 'We all agreed to put in a float of a hundred and fifty pounds each to start, and that allowed us to buy some starter shares. We all then set up monthly standing orders of thirty pounds each. This money went into a bank account, which was set up in the name of the share club. We had ten members, and we made sure that you needed at least four signatures to withdraw money in our share club bank account.

'Each week, if we all can, we sit down and work out what shares to buy. We each take responsibility for a particular sector. I looked at American technology stocks because I work in IT in the City.

'We made a bit of money at the beginning, but things then didn't do so well and we are a bit down financially. Still, we've enjoyed it so much that we're determined to keep the share club going. Until we all get broke.'

If you want to set up a share club, you'll need to contact a company called ProShare. They will send you a package with all you need to know about setting up share clubs.

HOW YOUR MONEY CAN CHANGE THE WORLD

OK, you may not have loads of cash, but if you want to do your bit to help the planet, and humankind, here are a few ideas you may wish to consider.

£   **pensions: lots of the funds have ethical options**
£   **electricity and gas: you can switch to a green tariff, and it could save you money**
£   **investing: ethical funds can be found in ISAs and unit trusts**
£   **charity: charities can claim back cash on all donations (see Your Working Life)**
£   **shares: find out the ethical policy of the company you are putting your cash into by ringing the Ethical Investment Research Service (EIRS – see Resources)**

If you are worried that ethical savings don't perform as well as nonethical investments, remember that, if more people refuse to put their money in companies that allow less than ethical practices, the more companies will have to rethink how they do make their money. Do you really want to make your cash at the expense of exploiting Third World countries?

MORE COMPLICATED AND RISKY INVESTMENTS

Learning about investing is not easy, but you can swot up on these.

FUTURES

Futures are a gamble on whether the prices of a commodity or a currency will go up or down. Futures are big business. A good or lucky futures trader can make thousands of pounds a day.

A futures trader will usually operate as a self-employed person, but will often rent space in an office where other futures traders work. Futures traders are regulated by the Securities and Futures Authority, which is part of the Financial Services Authority.

If there is such a thing as a fast buck to be made, then futures trading is probably the closest you'll get. Futures traders also tend to have the highest burnout rate in the City: the stress and pressures of having to make judgments involving thousands of pounds means the job tends to be a short-lived one.

HEDGE FUNDS

These are the most controversial kind of investment at the moment, as endowment policies were in the late 1990s. Basically, you are betting on whether shares will fall or rise. So a fund that bet that prices would fall in 2000, 2001 and 2002, for example, would have done very well. Thing is, a lot of hedge funds have bet that prices will rise, and that's where they have lost cash – sometimes lots of it. In fact, some hedge funds have sunk without a trace.

Hedge funds are not marketed in the UK. They are sold through word of mouth and not advertising and, because they are not regulated, they don't have to worry about how much they charge the people investing in them. But the biggest minus point is that you need around £90,000 to invest in them.

COMMODITIES

When finance people talk about these they are not talking about stocks or shares but about things that can actually be used. A commodity would be cocoa, coffee, gold, bananas.

The way that commodities are often used on the stock market is as a form of betting. You can offer to buy a futures contract in cocoa beans, betting that the price will be a certain level, and you then have the option to buy them at that point in time. If the price of cocoa beans when the futures contract expires is lower than you bet, then you've lost; if it's higher, then you've made cash because you can sell it on for more money.

CYCLICALS

This is a term used to describe stocks and or shares that have been around a long time, such as banks and medical firms. They are known as cyclicals because, even when they do badly, they soon get investors returning to buy them again.

BLUE-CHIP STOCK

The blue-chip companies are the largest ones listed on the stock exchange. In the UK's case blue-chip stocks would be those listed on the FTSE 100.

BEARS AND BULLS

People talk about a *bear market* when share prices are falling, so a bear is someone who expects share prices to fall. It also means the market is pessimistic.

The term *bull market* describes a market where shares are rising, so a bull is someone who expects share prices to rise. This kind of investor is also called *bullish*.

MUTUAL COMPANIES

Mutual companies are not listed on the stock exchange. When a company *demutualises* it is normally seeking such a listing.

When a company is *mutual* it is to all intents and purposes owned by the people who have accounts or financial products with it. Around the beginning of the 1990s building societies and life offices that had been mutual decided that they would be better off being owned by shareholders. So they asked all their account holders to vote on whether they should be listed on the stock market.

Lots of investors got windfalls, or shares, when the companies went to the stock market, companies such as Abbey National, Halifax and the Woolwich. There are still some mutual companies, such as Nationwide and the Co-operative Bank, and some life offices, such as Standard Life.

Building societies and mutual life offices have in recent years been clamping down on people who open accounts with building societies that they believe will demutualise. These people, known as carpetbaggers, hope to take advantage of any windfall to be made when the society demutualises.

OTHER IMPORTANT INFORMATION

What are premium bonds? If you really are looking for ways of multiplying your cash, then premium bonds might be your answer – if you get lucky that is. Premium bonds work like the National Lottery (now called the Lotto), except that there's only one draw a month. Each month a computer called Ernie will randomly pick a premium-bond number. The person owning that bond will receive £1 million – tax-free. There are also lots of smaller prizes, from £50 upwards.

The minimum amount you need to buy a premium bond is £100. The chances of winning are higher than those of the Lotto, but those who buy premium bonds tend to be rich people who buy up sometimes hundreds of thousands of pounds' worth. Premium bonds are a good way of keeping your cash working, as you can get your money back at any time, but remember that they don't earn interest. You don't pay tax when you get your cash back because you've already paid tax, via income tax, on the money you bought the bonds with.

Can I really trust the stock market? The advice here is to use caution at all times. Jenny, a mother of two, says, 'I had some LastMinute.com shares. The opening offer was so oversubscribed, such was the demand for the shares. But as soon as the company was floated the shares started to dive right down. It seemed to be a real case of greed. Now, though, they've done OK and are actually one of the best-performing shares. The fact is they sell cheap holidays and at the end of the day people are always going to want to go on holiday.'

What about collective investments? If you want to buy a collective investment and you are not sure which ones to pick, visit a financial adviser who is trained to offer investment advice (not all of them are, so check with IFA Promotion first). Your first visit will probably be free and they will ask you to fill out a questionnaire that will work out your risk profile – this will give the adviser an idea of whether you are prepared, or can afford, to put your money into what are considered the more risky investments.

Can I go it alone? Yes, you can. In the last couple of years more and more investment companies have set up sites – execution-only – on the Internet. These allow you to pick and choose the kinds of investment you want in your portfolio. There are also sites that have fund supermarkets – these allow you to shop around. But you really have to know what you want first.

What's the difference between a financial adviser and a fund manager? A financial adviser is responsible for selling you the fund. For this they may take a commission as well, but this will normally be paid to them out of the initial charge. A fund manager is the person responsible for deciding the makeup of the fund. You can buy the collective investments from fund managers.

What's an investment house? This is a broad term applied to all the companies that specialise in selling the unit trusts. The financial adviser is the middleman selling the products of the company. There are companies, for example Fidelity and a number of small Scottish investment companies, that manage only funds, while most of the banks and building societies have their own specialist investment divisions.

INVESTMENT POINTS TO REMEMBER

You'll have come across pieces of advice throughout this book, and some of it is repeated here, but you can never have too much of it. So keep in mind these essential points.

- £ **Cash-based investments are safer but you may not make much from them.**
- £ **Shares go up and down, and when you really need them to go up, they go down.**
- £ **Follow your gut feelings, but do your homework first.**
- £ **Nothing is guaranteed, but some investments are safer than others.**
- £ **If your investment makes money it should be an unexpected bonus.**
- £ **If times get tough, you may be better looking at fixed-rate investments like government bonds.**
- £ **Always get advice when you start out.**

If your brain isn't too fried then you may, just may, want to check out the following helpful people.

The Association of Investment Trust Companies (AITC) will be more than happy to give you information on investment trusts. You can browse the website on www.itsonline.co.uk or contact the association on 08000 858520. AITC is based at Durrant House (3rd Floor), 8–13 Chiswell Street, London EC1Y 4YY.

Association of Unit Trusts and Investment Funds (AUTIF), who are at 65 Kingsway, London WC2B 6TD, can give information on ISAs, OEICs and exchange-traded funds, as well as unit trusts. The phone number is 020 8207 1361 and the website is www.investmentfunds.org.uk.

The London Stock Exchange has fact sheets on buying and selling shares and even information about the exchange itself. The number is 020 7797 1000 and the website is www.londonstockexchange.com. The LSE is based at the Public Information Department, Old Broad Street, London EC2N 1HP.

Buying shares The Association of Private Client Investment Managers and Stockbrokers (APCIMS) provides a free directory of stockbrokers (share dealers) and investment managers in the UK. Contact them on 020 7247 7080. The website is www.apcims.org.uk.

Setting up a share club ProShare (UK) Ltd, at Centurion House, 24 Monument Street, London EC3R 8AR, helps you get a share club started. Call 020 7220 1730 or log on at www.proshare.org.uk.

Going green Find out who provides ethical investments, savings and pensions from the Ethical Investment Research Service (EIRiS) on 020 7840 5700 or www.eiris.org, or call 0845 606 0324 to get in touch with financial advisers who specialise in ethical savings.

Buying gilts You can buy gilts by post through the Bank of England Brokerage Service. A free booklet, *Investing in Gilts – the Private Investor's Guide to British Government Stocks*, gives details on how to buy and sell gilts. It is available from the Debt Management Office on 020 7862 6525 or their website at www.dmo.gov.uk.

10 THE END – KIND OF ...

We couldn't leave you hanging like that. Here's a quick and easy guide to financial nirvana, reflecting the structure of this book. It will also be a useful reference tool to guide you back to the appropriate chapter if you want to revisit that information.

SPENDING

£ Check your bank account – it may be worth swapping to a better one.
£ Are you paying too much interest on your credit card? If so, shop around for another, or pay it off fast.
£ Always check the APR of a loan, even if it claims to be interest-free for the first six months.
£ Learn how to budget on the small stuff so you can spend on the large things.

DEBT

£ Never borrow from family or friends if you don't mean to pay it back.
£ Accept that some things, such as being a student, may involve a bit of debt.
£ You won't get jailed for being in debt to a bank or building society ...
£ ... but it can give you sleepless nights, so, if you are in trouble, talk to someone.

SAVING

£ Even if it is a small amount you want to save, open a cash ISA.
£ Teach youngsters the value of money.
£ Have your money where you can get at it in an emergency ...
£ ... but don't have it too close to hand!

RELATIONSHIPS

£ If you are flat sharing, have a household budget.
£ If you are living with a partner, have your own bank account.
£ Always make a will, whether you are married or not.
£ Make friends with your solicitor – you may need them one day.

PROTECTING

£   Don't take out every insurance under the sun – some cover the same thing.

£   If you have a car, always shop around for insurance.

£   There are always things you can do to make your insurance cheaper.

£   Learn more about medical insurance – it can be complicated.

WORKING

£   Know your tax code, and know how much tax you pay.

£   Always read your contract of employment.

£   Make sure you get everything you are entitled to.

£   Don't be afraid to ask for extra perks.

NESTING

£   You don't *have* to buy a house – not everyone can cope with a mortgage.

£   The right time to buy is the right time for you.

£   Shop around for a mortgage – they are not all the same.

£   If you rent, make sure you have a signed agreement with your landlord.

GETTING OLD

£   If you don't have a pension, have lots of savings (if you want to grow old, that is).

£   You are never too old to start saving for old age.

£   Pensions are not that complicated – it's the tax laws that are.

£   Shop around for a pension – they are not all the same.

MAKING MORE

£   Shares are not a good buy if you are broke.

£   If you do have spare cash, spread your risk.

£   In tough times think about buying gilts.

£   Always, always read the small print and, if you don't understand it, get someone to explain it to you.

207

RESOURCES

Here is a summary of the important numbers you'll need, plus a few others. Some of them are helplines, while others will give you more specialised information.

FINANCIAL SERVICES

The government body in charge of making sure that most financial products you buy are above board and that the firms that sell them are properly qualified to do so is the Financial Services Authority (FSA); it also operates a register that can tell you which firms are authorised to sell financial products:

The Financial Services Authority
25 North Colonnade
Canary Wharf
London E14 5HS
Consumer helpline 0845 606 1234
www.fsa.gov.uk
Email consumerhelp@fsa.gov.uk.

BUYING SHARES

The Association of Private Client Investment Managers and Stockbrokers (APCIMS) provides a free directory of stockbrokers (share dealers) and investment managers in the UK:

The Association of Private Client Investment Managers and Stockbrokers
3rd Floor
112 Middlesex Street
London
E1 7HY
020 7247 7080
www.apcims.org.uk.

GOING GREEN

Find out who provides ethical investments, savings and pension from:

Ethical Investment Research Service (EIRiS)
80 Bondway
London
SW8 1SG
020 7840 5700 (or 0845 606 0324 to get in touch with financial advisers who specialise in ethical products)
www.eiris.org.

FINDING AN ADVISER

Get details of local financial experts in your area:

IFA Promotion
113-117 Farringdon Road
London
EC1R 3BT
0117 971 1177
www.unbiased.co.uk.

There's also a *Money Management* (the magazine aimed at financial advisers) national register of fee-based advisers on 0870 013 1925.

FINANCIAL ADVICE

Solicitors for Independent Financial Advice (for solicitors who also deal with legal matters such as pensions and divorce)
10 East Street
Epsom
Surrey KT17 1HH
01372 721172
www.sifa.co.uk.

The Society for Financial Advisers
Aldermanbury
London EC2V 7HY
020 7417 4419

The Association of Independent Financial Advisers
020 7628 1287
www.aifa.net.

GETTING LEGAL ADVICE

The Law Society
Law Society's Hall
113 Chancery Lane
London WC2 1PL
020 7242 1222
www.lawsociety.org.uk.

The Law Society of Northern Ireland
Law Society House
98 Victoria Street
Belfast BT1 3JZ
028 9023 1614
www.lawsoc-ni.org.

The Law Society of Scotland
Law Society's Hall
26 Drumasleugh Gardens
Edinburgh EH3 7YR
020 7417 4419
www.lawscot.org.uk.

MONEY WORRIES?

Citizens' Advice Bureau
(see your local phone book)

The Consumers' Association
2 Marylebone Road
London
NW1 4DF

The Consumers' Association is very useful for all aspects of saving
and spending. You can order its books via 0800 252100.

BENEFITS

The Department of Work and Pensions – order free fact sheets on benefits by phoning 0345 313233.

MORTGAGES

The Council of Mortgage Lenders can provide copies of the Mortgage Code:

The Council of Mortgage Lenders
3 Savile Row
London W1X 1AF
020 7437 0075.
The Arbitration Service is contactable through the same address.

The banks, building societies and other mortgage lenders who subscribe to it can be found by phoning:

The Mortgage Code Compliance Board
Festival Way
Festival Park
Stoke-on-Trent
Staffordshire ST1 5TA
01782 216300.

TAX

For details of your tax office, check your P45.

The Inland Revenue
PO Box 37
St Austell
Cornwall PL25 5YN
0845 900 0404
www.inlandrevenue.gov.uk.

PENSIONS

OPRA, or the Occupational Pension Regulatory Authority, makes sure that the money put into workplace pension schemes does not go AWOL:

Occupational Pension Regulatory Authority
Invicta House
Trafalgar Place
Brighton BN1 4DW
01273 627600
www.opra.co.uk.

COMPLAINTS

The Financial Services Compensation Scheme
7th Floor
Lloyds Chambers
1 Portsoken Street
London E1 8BN
020 7892 7300
www.fscs.org.uk
(there are limits on how much compensation you can claim)

If the firm you have the complaint against is still trading you should get in touch with:

The Financial Ombudsman Scheme
South Quay Plaza
183 Marsh Wall
London E14 9SR
0845 080 1800
www.financial-ombudsman.org.uk.

CREDITS

The material in this book is not intended as advice: it is intended to inspire. If you have any more questions about your own finances I would strongly advise you to seek the help of one of the listed experts.

And remember, if it's too good to be true and it involves money, it probably is.

CHAPTERS 1 AND 2: SPENDING AND DEBT

Latest financial information on student loans was taken from *Students' Money Matters*, 2002, by Gwenda Thomas, supported by UCAS, (Trotman, ISBN 0 85660 811 4).

The Financial Services Authority's website, www.fsa.gov.uk, provided the useful addresses.

The Community Legal Services Commission with Consumers' Association and Birmingham Settlement – leaflet No. 1, 'Dealing with Debt', April 2001.

www.legalservices.gov.uk.

CHAPTER 3: SAVING

The current ISA saving limits were checked with the Inland Revenue website.

CHAPTER 4: RELATIONSHIPS

The extremely useful 'prenuptial' information was inspired by an excellent financial adviser, Ruth Whitehead of Ruth Whitehead Associates, for a guide I compiled for women about to enter relationships (in June 2001). We are often told that prenuptials are not worth the paper they are written on, but Ruth disagreed: she showed me how important it was to have something down on paper.

CHAPTER 5: PROTECTION

The latest information on health and life insurance came from the Association of British Insurers' consumer helpline, on 020 7600 3333, and from their website, www.abi.org.uk.

CHAPTER 6: WORKING LIFE

Paula Twigg at the Child Poverty Action Group helped me with the details on the maximum-working-week directive.

CHAPTER 7: BUILDING A NEST

Staff at the Bishop's Stortford branches of Abbey National, Bradford & Bingley, Halifax and HSBC gave the latest information on the mortgage market. Staff at Nockolds Solicitors provided information on what makes a common-law couple.

CHAPTER 8: GETTING OLD

The Equitable Life update was helped by an article on BBC News Online: 'Equitable plans misselling payouts', dated 30 September 2002.

Lowe, Jonquil, *The Which? Guide to Planning Your Pension, 2002* (Which Books, ISBN 0 85202 901 2).

CHAPTER 9: MAKING POTS MORE (MAYBE)

The Financial Services Authority website and the latest Inland Revenue website were consulted for the latest details on the state of the investment market. The London Stock Exchange provided help with material on stockbrokers.

FURTHER READING

Rowe, Dorothy, *The Real Meaning of Money*, HarperCollins (pbk), 1998

Inman, Colin, *The FT Style Guide*, Prentice Hall (pbk), 2000

ACKNOWLEDGEMENTS

A special thank-you to my 'team' of financial experts, including Marianne Kelly, whose financial expertise helped me overcome my tendency to say, 'Oh my God, what else have I missed?' To my mum (and personal assistant) Jacqui Kinnison, my sister Katie and brother-in-law John, and poor Peter, who got the brunt of every temper tantrum when my PC was too slow, coffee was too cold, or house was too hot.

Thanks to Annalise for making me realise that real priorities are not just about money.

Thanks, too, to all the regular users, not fair-weather folk like me, of Bishop's Stortford and Harlow libraries for putting up with me when my battery-hungry laptop had a tantrum.

To all the interviewees: I've changed your names but you know who you are. Thanks.

Much gratitude also to Alex Shakespeare, Hellie Ieronimo, Paula Twigg and Mandy Charles.

Thanks to the yoga crew and to dear, dear Margie Pope. Thanks for the regular cups of good karma.

And finally, thanks to the credit cards I've loved, lost and now manage successfully.

INDEX